A gift for:

From:

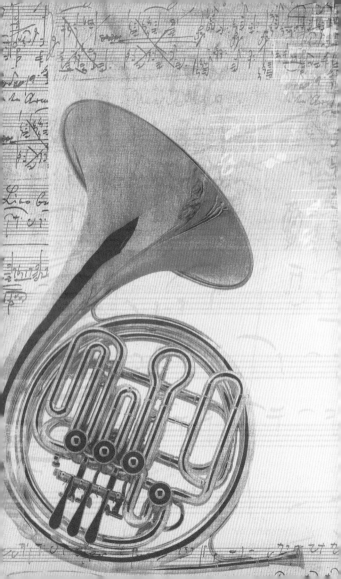

Praise

IN THE PRESENCE OF GOD

A Daily Celebration

JACK HAYFORD

www.jcountryman.com
A division of Thomas Nelson, Inc.
www.thomasnelson.com

www.thomasnelson.com
www.jcountryman.com

Designed by UDG|DesignWorks, Sisters, Oregon.

ISBN: 1-4041-0083-0

Printed and bound in Belgium

To Anna . . .
with whom this year
I celebrate fifty years of walking together
in the love of Jesus—hand in hand,
serving Him and His people.

PREFACE

Praise is a pathway—

Walk there daily, whatever you feel, for praise is more than an experience—it shapes what our experiences will become. Praise not only exclaims God's worthiness, it is a privilege that invokes His daily mercies, grace, and power into our lives.

As the day's path unfolds, speak praises—for praise invites heaven's sunlight into life's circumstances and crowds out all darkness. And at times, set your pace with songs of praise—sung, hummed, or whistled. Harmonize your heart with heaven and watch God's hand reach into your world.

Never leave the pathway of praise—

When doubts come, praise God that His Word will never fail you.

When fears taunt, praise God that His presence never leaves you.

When questions arise, praise God that His wisdom holds every answer.

May this book become a daily companion; a guide pointing each day's footsteps along the one road that assures peace beyond strife, hope beyond trial, joy beyond sorrow, and life beyond all—unto an eternity of praising Him who loved us and gave Himself for us.

—Jack Hayford

Spirit of God, unfold the Word,

Thy deepest secrets let me discern. . . .

Teach of Thy Cross, and liberate me.

January

TRUE LOVE

FOR GOD

BEGINS WITH

DELIGHT IN

HIS HOLINESS.

GOD WITH HIS PEOPLE

Who may stand in His holy place?
He who has clean hands and a pure heart.

PSALM 24:3–4

 David was more than the kid who killed a giant. He was a real person who endured incredible difficulty and rose beyond impossible odds, raised by God almighty Himself to become king of Israel. David was a man who understood God's heart.

It was not only David's reverence for the awesome majesty of the Almighty that produced his understanding of the Lord, but also his insight into God's desire for intimacy. He knew God wanted to dwell with His people—up close, in every heart, with every family, in every home.

Glory on Your House

SON OF THE LIVING GOD

You are the Christ, the Son of the living God.

MATTHEW 16:16

These words are rich with meaning, giving clear definition to what Simon had come to believe about Jesus. It's a complete declaration of faith.

You are Christ—that is to say: "*Jesus,* You're the Messiah, the anticipated King of glory, the promised One."

The Son—that is to say: "*Jesus,* You are God-become-flesh, the Word from eternity incarnate in time."

Of the living God—that is to say: "*Jesus,* You are God! You are more than a superhuman, more than an exceedingly wonderful teacher, more than the sum of humanity's highest potential. You are the Creator of all things come to be the Redeemer of all mankind."

The Power and Blessing

LEARNING TO WORSHIP

You will show me the path of life;
in Your presence is fullness of joy.

PSALM 16:11

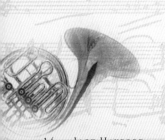 C. S. Lewis wrote in *Reflections on the Psalms,* "I think we delight to praise what we enjoy because the praise not merely expresses but completes the enjoyment. It is not out of compliment that lovers keep on telling one another how beautiful they are; the delight is incomplete till it is expressed."

We cannot praise God until we delight in Him and love Him. We cannot do those things until we know Him intimately. We cannot know Him intimately until we spend time with Him.

Living the Spirit-Formed Life

PREPARED FOR THE KING

*Lift up your heads, O you gates! Lift up, you
everlasting doors! And the King of glory shall come in.*

PSALM 24:9

Throughout the Psalms there is an interplay
between David, king of Israel, and, in a prophetic
sense, Christ—the King from whom David received
his own throne. In Psalm 24 the rich imagery is of
a great king approaching his city. As he and his
colorful entourage approach the city gates, their
presence is so commanding that the gates—the city
leaders gathered in counsel—are exhorted to attend
to their entry. The city and its inhabitants are to
make the royal party welcome.

David proposes a royal welcome for the King
of heaven. Are the gates to our hearts prepared to
give such honor to the entry and enthronement of
Christ, our King? Let every ear hear it! Let every
heart-gate open freely for His entry.

The Heart of Praise

MORE THAN MERRIMENT

Ask, and you will receive,
that your joy may be full.

JOHN 16:24

 Joy is more than merriment, more than happiness, and more than the other myriad of human expressions and experiences we use to describe happy fulfillment. Joy includes them all, but transcends them by leagues.

Joy is the certainty that whatever leashes your life to less than Love, or whatever has stained your soul with shame or failure has been neutralized by the one power that can free and forgive us all—the living Christ.

Come . . . and Behold Him!

THE REALITY OF GOD

*In Him dwells all the fullness of the
Godhead bodily; and you are complete in Him.*

COLOSSIANS 2:9

Jesus came to teach us clearly what the Father is like. He is the precise revelation of God's nature, in contrast to the images that human imagination sometimes projects!

Distorted images of "father" often haunt us; humanly fallible authority figures sour our view of God. But shedding His light and dispelling the shadows of confusion, Jesus visits us to show how the eternal Father expresses authority and love in equal balance. We see the complete reality of God in Jesus, for "in Him dwells all the fullness of God" (paraphrase).

The Visitor

It's Up to You and Me

He who follows righteousness and
mercy finds life, righteousness and honor.

PROVERBS 21:21

Our relationships with one another are not administrated by God. If another person is going to be forgiven for overlooking something that inconvenienced me, God isn't going to do it. I have to do it.

What will motivate me to do that, especially if I don't like (1) what happened, (2) how I was accused, (3) the argument that was thrown at me or (4) the inconvenience of injustice I suffered? I will only forgive when I remember how vastly greater than my frustration or pain are the dimensions of God's forgiveness toward me. That's the key.

The Key to Everything

POSSESS THE PROMISE

*Go over this Jordan . . . to the land which
I am giving. . . . Every place that the sole of your foot
will tread upon I have given you.*

JOSHUA 1:2–3

 The promise is pregnant with divine possibility, yet integrated with human responsibility. Clearly the Lord was saying to Joshua (1) He had already gone before with a plan and by His power, but (2) the "possessing" was Joshua's part: "Reach out, and take it." God knew what Joshua's tomorrow would hold, but He made Joshua responsible to stride out—to possess the tomorrows of divine promise.

Taking Hold of Tomorrow

THE COMFORTER

I will pray the Father, and He will give you
another Helper, that He may abide with you forever.

JOHN 14:16

In Australia, there's a tree called the *Jarrah*—also known as "ironwood." This tree is so heavy and dense and hard that termites hate it. That's why this ironwood is used widely in construction. But let me tell you, it takes real strength, skill, and determination to build with ironwood.

Aspects of your life may cause you to wonder: *Is this a "jarrah" situation—one so hard I don't think I'll ever be able to "cut it"?*

Well, rest in comfort—rather, in the Comforter. The Holy Spirit can handle it! He is deeply personal, all-powerful, and ever present. And He wants to make Himself known in the details of your life and your relationships.

Rebuilding the Real You

WEAKNESS FOR STRENGTH

*I bow my knees to the Father of our
Lord Jesus Christ, from whom the whole family
in heaven and earth is named.*

EPHESIANS 3:14–15

God's holiness sets Him apart from all of His creatures—angelic, human, and animal. In the beauty of His holiness, He commits to make His worshipers holy, too. He forgives our sins, . . . He sanctifies us, He conforms us to the image of His only begotten Son.

We don't become holy by matching up our strength to God's. We match up our weakness to His strength and our failure to His holiness, so that our lives may reflect His righteousness and glory.

Living the Spirit-Formed Life

RESTORATION

*I will restore to you the years
that the swarming locust has eaten.*

JOEL 2:25

Just as any loving parent would be, God is injured and grieved when, through rebellion or ignorance, any of us pursues our own way to our own destruction. Yet His judgment is never vindictive. In fact, for the most part, God doesn't even have to activate most instances of judgment upon sin. The vast majority of human sinning carries within itself the deadly seeds of its own penalty. As wondrous as our eternal salvation is, coming to the Savior does not immediately dissolve the long-term damage to our souls caused by sin.

Knowing Christ brings us in touch with the Holy Spirit—God's restoration resource—for dealing with the residue of sin. The Holy Spirit offers us the help we need for supernatural recovery and the rebuilding of our minds and emotions.

Rebuilding the Real You

CERTAINTY OF PRAYER

*Casting all your care
upon Him, for He cares for you.*

1 PETER 5:7

You've hit a blockade on the highway to happiness.

You're face-to-face with an impossibility—or what seems like it.

Everybody gets to this point at some time. Positive thinking disappears, from all but the most tenacious. Faith dims for all except the most rock-like saint. At this point you're ready for an answer.

You're ready to pray—to pray as an entrance into reality, to pray as a trip with predestined certainty, to pray as an experience of intelligently based peace, to pray with the knowledge you're on target every time.

Prayer Is Invading Impossible

JOURNEY OF FAITH

I am the way, the truth, and the life.

JOHN 14:6

Jesus—Who is "the Way"—is always calling us to follow Him. Reading the journals of Faith's champions, we find that to effectively and fruitfully follow Christ is to follow a lifelong summons to new horizons. There's a certain unsettledness with any serious disciple. It isn't the unsettledness of erratic faith or behavior, but an unpredictability—a readiness to "go where You want me to go, dear Lord . . . be what You want me to be."

Since Abraham, the first to "go out, not knowing where," the faith-life has always been described as a journey—a pilgrimage. It reflects a flexibility of soul that refuses to limit itself to know the truth—it insists on *experiencing* it as well.

A Passion for Fullness

RELENTLESS LOVE

*Let Your hand become
my help, for I have chosen Your precepts.*

PSALM 119:173

Each of us has the terrible capacity to slam the door in the face of God's promises. Not just promises for salvation and eternal life but promises for our lives, for our families, for our businesses, for our relationships, for our weaknesses, for our torment, for our bondage.

Yet, God's love is relentless. We may lock ourselves up in anxiety, distress, perplexity, and grief. But when we call upon Him, Jesus moves right into our situation, shut doors and all. He is in no way reluctant to step into our deepest confusion and despair, bringing comfort, healing, and deliverance.

Glorious Morning!

WORSHIP-FILLED PRAISE

Lord, teach us to pray.

LUKE 11:1

Jesus points us toward the pathway of worship-filled praise when He says (and I paraphrase freely):

1. *Our Father in heaven* (and I thank You for that relationship You have given me through Your Son, my Savior),

2. *Hallowed be Your name* (for You are holy, and I worship You and revel in the beauty of Your completeness and excellence),

3. *Your Kingdom come* (for there is no rule of my wisdom or of human working that can bring about Your peace, power, and blessing);

4. *Your will be done* (because I bow in full submission to declare, as did Your Son, "Not My will but Yours be done"),

5. *On earth as it is in heaven* (for there is no question Your will is exercised where Your throne is established).

Glory on Your House

CHRIST'S CREATIVE WORD

In the beginning was the Word. . . .
All things were made through Him, and without
Him nothing was made that was made.

JOHN 1:1, 3

 He who spoke all things into existence continues by the sheer power of His creative word to sustain them in existence.

When He speaks a promise, it can be believed. When He declares a goal concerning His work and His will for His redeemed, we can depend on His bringing it about. Loved one, if He can sustain all creation by His own word, we can rest assured He'll see us through when He says He will! Hallelujah!

The Visitor

GIVING "GIVINGLY"

With the same measure that
you use, it will be measured back to you.

LUKE 6:38

The principle of Luke 6:38 applies to every area of life.

People don't have friends because they don't offer friendship.

People can't establish pure relationships because they don't apply God's pure terms to the conduct of the relationships they're pursuing.

People don't feel forgiven because they won't give forgiveness.

People don't find contentment because they won't accept God's providence.

The principle of reciprocity—of an expected return for giving—is God's idea for expanding life's dimensions through giving. Giving money, giving kindness, giving time, giving up, giving in, giving "givingly"!

The Key to Everything

BEING BRIDGES

Love suffers long and is kind.

1 CORINTHIANS 13:4

God ministers to every individual with a perfect knowledge of each person's needs. While He will certainly understand my hurt feelings and comfort me when I have been mistreated, He will also be concerned with all that is happening to and in the other person.

I may consider the other person my adversary, but Jesus cares as much about that person's needs as He does about mine. And He wants me to learn this and open my heart to being used by Him to bridge rifts in relationships.

Our Daily Walk

HEARTFELT REPENTANCE

You do not delight in burnt offering.
The sacrifices of God are a broken spirit,
a broken and a contrite heart.

PSALM 51:16–17

Remember the depth of David's sin with Bathsheba and his gross attempt to cover it up with the murder of her husband Uriah? As a wealthy king, David could offer thousands of oxen or sheep or goats on the altar before God. But there weren't enough animals in the world to compensate for his sin. It was David's heart that had been closed to the will of God. It was David's heart that had to break in repentance.

The sacrifice God really wants is a broken heart. Ultimately, it's not the sight of an animal sacrifice that moves God to grant forgiveness. It's a broken heart—a spirit grown tender enough to be pained by sin.

The Heart of Praise

THE PRIVILEGE OF PRAISE

My soul shall be joyful in my God; for He
has clothed me with the garments of salvation.

ISAIAH 61:10

Worship is for God. It is birthed by His gift of life to us and His great love for us. Worship is due Him and entirely for Him.

Sing happily, rejoice openly, cry humbly, shout triumphantly, praise unreservedly. Let us come before His throne with a full sense of His worthiness and a judicious sense of our happy privilege to be invited.

In God's order, worship brings our total being aglow in the life the Holy Spirit imparts, enabling us to offer spiritual sacrifices.

Glory on Your House

HUMBLED BY GOD'S LOVE

I dwell in the high and holy place,
with him who has a contrite and humble spirit.

ISAIAH 57:15

There is nothing more humbling than discovering how deeply we are loved.

I'm persuaded that true humility lies in our (1) *receiving* simply God's high purpose, (2) *living* it in His will, and (3) *serving* the interests of others.

God has created us in His image.

He has redeemed us at the inestimable price of Christ's blood.

He has poured the treasure of His Holy Spirit into our lives.

With all that investment, it's no small wonder He declares His will to do great and marvelous things with each of us!

Taking Hold of Tomorrow

LETTERS OF AUTHORITY

Whatever you ask in My name, that
I will do, that the Father may be glorified in the Son.

JOHN 14:14

When Jesus ascended to heaven, He expressed at least two promises of far-reaching significance: (1) He would build a Church and (2) He would give the Church authority to act in His name. He further made clear that the Holy Spirit's coming would provide the power to accomplish these tasks.

As participants in His building process, we need to understand the authority the Spirit has brought us. "Whatsoever you ask in my name," Jesus said, "the Father will do it for you." And, "All authority has been given to Me in heaven and on earth" (Matt. 28:18).

These credentials—the privilege of praying and operating in the name of Jesus—are letters of authority pressed into your hand by Christ the King.

Rebuilding the Real You

GOD'S WAYS OR MINE?

Find out what pleases the Lord.

EPHESIANS 5:10, NIV

Sooner or later we need to come to terms with this dilemma: God's ways . . . or mine? Wisdom recommends we learn to align ourselves with God's thoughts and ways. It is crucial not only to our growth as believers, but to our fulfillment as the Father's children. I need to teach myself to say, "Yes, this seems like a good and sensible course of action on the surface . . . but what does the Father have to say? What is His mind on this thing?"

His word of promise, His law of wisdom, and His Spirit's prompting within—when allowed reign over and above my mind—have a way of nudging me beyond the limits of human "sense" toward the horizons of holy "hope."

A New Time and Place

EXCELLENCE AND GLORY

It is . . . God . . . who has shone in our hearts
to give the light of the knowledge of the glory of God
in the face of Jesus Christ.

2 CORINTHIANS 4:6

 Residing in every human heart are dreams of glory. Although the realities of life and the limitations of our flesh tend to quench our desire to attain those dreams, Christ has come to bring every one of us into His glory.

Jesus presented the ultimate of God's excellence. He is the best. He cannot be excelled. He is a complete picture of excellence, of all that we who are in Him can hope to become.

Living and Praying in Jesus' Name

KNOWING GOD

I will meditate on Your precepts,
and contemplate Your ways.

PSALM 119:15

As we study the Scriptures we see a growing revelation of God's heart toward us and His purpose for us. At each encounter with every individual, God is seeking to reveal more of Himself. The purpose of His revelation is that we may more deeply know Him.

Knowing God is the primary purpose of all mankind—to know Him intimately, to know His heart, to know how He thinks, to know His personal interest in us, to know the economy of His dealings—how He relates.

The Bible unfolds so much regarding God's character, His nature, and His disposition of love toward us, that none of us needs to experience anything less than a full and intimate relationship with Him.

Grounds for Living

GROWING DISCIPLES

Take My yoke upon you and learn from Me . . .
and you will find rest for your souls.

MATTHEW 11:29

 Discipleship is the call to Calvary, first and foremost to receive the forgiveness and salvation provided by God's great love. But we are never to remain solely as forgiven penitents. We are called to grow as God's sons and daughters, to serve as His faithful stewards, to learn as His devoted disciples. And all of that growth, service, and learning is most practically processed not by the way we handle life's blessings, but by the way we live through its bad days.

How to Live Through a Bad Day

A Spirit of Praise

I will bless the LORD at all times;
His praise shall continually be in my mouth.

PSALM 34:1

Over the years, I've become convinced that praise sets up a mantle of protection around the people of God. Praise is an atmosphere through which the Adversary cannot move.

If you and I really entered into this truth, it would transform our lives. And it's not simply because praise can insulate or protect us. It's more than that. It's because *God is worthy,* . . . worthy of the best of our praise, the depths of our thanksgiving. As you ask the Lord to teach you more and more about the tireless, ongoing spirit of praise, it will change your circumstances, and it will change you!

Moments with Majesty

GOD IN THE DETAILS

*If we walk in the light as He is in the light,
we have fellowship with one another, and the blood of
Jesus Christ His Son cleanses us from all sin.*

1 JOHN 1:7

 Our total acceptance before the Father is no substitute for the fact that He is calling us to His holiness—that is, the restoration of our souls and the wholeness of our personalities.

We can't be any more accepted than we already are as His children. We can't be any more victorious than we already are in the dominion He's given us over the power of the enemy.

But we can become progressively more whole—holy—in the practical details of daily living.

Rebuilding the Real You

BLESSINGS ON EARTH

Blessings are on the head of the righteous, but
violence covers the mouth of the wicked.

PROVERBS 10:6

You and I can help decide which of these two things—blessing or cursing—happen on earth. We will determine whether God's goodness is released toward specific situations or whether the power of sin and Satan is permitted to prevail.

Prayer is the determining factor.

Since only the light of Calvary's power can dissipate the darkness of the workings of hell, the only people who can reverse the tide of encroaching evil, wherever it rises, are those who pray in Jesus' name.

Prayer Is Invading the Impossible

"Do You Love Me?"

Lord, You know all things; You know that I love You.

JOHN 21:17

Christ has a way not only of calling us to serve His purposes, but of calling us to unfamiliar environments that require new trust and dependence on Him. That stretches us to deeper levels of character.

The primary thing Jesus wants to know about you and me is simply this: "Do you love Me?" Because if that love is in place, however fragile our sense of our own capabilities may be, He can take us from there!

And moreover, He can take us farther than we ever dreamed!

Remember that in serving Him, everything flows out of "first love": loving Jesus first, and following Jesus ever. It's the ultimate discipline. And it always bears the fullest fruit.

The Power and Blessing

PURSUIT OF PRAISE

Let the LORD be glorified, that we may see your joy.

ISAIAH 66:5

Praise is not intended to compliment God. Some people have confessed quite candidly that praise seems like an effort to curry God's favor by soothing or massaging His heavenly ego.

But praise is not the blind pursuit of heavenly intervention. It is an instrument of violence. It upsets the climate that furthers life's suffering, confusion, turmoil, and strife.

Praise destroys the atmosphere in which sickness, disease, discouragement, and futility flourish.

Praise beats out hell's brush fires and breathes heaven's life into death's vacuum.

Prayer Is Invading the Impossible

February

THE HONOR
AND GLORY
BELONG UNTO THEE,
THE WISDOM AND
POWER AND
ALL MAJESTY.

FULFILLER OF DREAMS

Your sons and daughters will prophesy, your young men will see visions, your old men will dream dreams.

ACTS 2:17, NIV

Hold your dreams in hands of faith, kept open before the living Lord who alone is the fulfiller of dreams.

Receive your dream—*talk* in a way that does not dissipate it.

Pursue your dream—*walk* in a way that does not violate it.

I can be sure my dream comes from God, when it is conceived of the beautiful, righteous, and profitable, and is rooted in truth and fulfilled through obedience and discipline.

Keep your dream in view. It is the will of God that you do!

Pastors of Promise

PATHWAY OF PRAISE

I will glorify the house of My glory.

ISAIAH 60:7

 Where people worship God humbly, forthrightly, and obediently, according to His Word, He will respond with a distinct show of His presence. Worship-filled praise invites the rule of His glorious Kingdom, and He enters with loving blessings and liberating power. Honoring God's Word in our lives, exalting God's Son with our lips, and giving the Holy Spirit a place to work by the love we show God and one another allow distinct and marvelous blessings to pour forth.

His glory may become the increasing portion of anyone who pursues a pathway of humility before His throne.

Glory on Your House

HUMBLY AND HONESTLY

*I have not come to call
the righteous, but sinners, to repentance.*

LUKE 5:32

The essence of sin is not so much in the *action* of sinning as it is in the *source* of sinning: self-centeredness and fear-filled self-protection. When our fears seek to mask our inadequacies, pride takes over. Pretended self-sufficiency eventually leads to self-righteousness, and arrogance forces its rule of vanity as we grow to believe our own lies. But when we fall before Jesus, humbly and honestly, there is nothing—personal weakness, inadequacy, failure, sinfulness—from which He cannot cleanse or deliver us.

Our Daily Walk

REBUILT BY THE SPIRIT

If anyone is in Christ, he is a new creation.

2 CORINTHIANS 5:17

Many believers have such a struggle trying to learn to walk as steadfast disciples of Christ while still crippled from their pasts. Although in sincerity they seek to speed ahead, before long they become frustrated and confused, especially when they see others who are progressing steadily.

But to become a new creature in Christ is only the beginning of this new life. The promise, "If anyone is in Christ, he is a new creation," does not instantly guarantee completed products. It does promise new possibilities opening to us—we are no longer dominated or controlled by our pasts. But for the full dominion of Christ's rule to penetrate the whole personality, in most cases "the real you" needs to be rebuilt by the Spirit, day by day by day.

Rebuilding the Real You

GOD'S LEADING

Blessed are the pure in heart, for they shall see God.

MATTHEW 5:8

 If we will only listen, God will teach us and refine our walk along the pathway of purity. But we must come with an open heart, ready to listen and let the Father "check up" on our daily words and actions. Daybreak is the best starting point for this checkup. Learning to invite the Lord to search our hearts can protect us from many future problems. When we abandon ourselves—our thoughts, motives, ambitions, and plans—to God's scrutiny, we open ourselves to His leading in every decision of our lives, great or small.

Our Daily Walk

A FORMIDABLE FUTURE

Pray without ceasing. . . . He who
calls you is faithful, who also will do it.

1 THESSALONIANS 5:17, 24

The impossible faces us all.
It storms, fumes,
looms before us,
stalks our days,
presses upon our minds,
bends our plans,
stands formidably across our future,
pierces our present,
reaches out from the past.

THERE IS A WAY TO FACE IMPOSSIBILITY—
INVADE IT!
Not with a glib speech of high hopes,
not in anger,
not with resignation.
not through stoical self-control,
but with prayer.

Prayer Is Invading the Impossible

A PASSION FOR GOD

I will meditate on the glorious splendor
of Your majesty, and on Your wondrous works.

PSALM 145:5

God is far more interested in our personal passion for Him than He is in our academic perceptions about Him.

I'm not indifferent toward the value of systematic theology, or solidly grounded understanding but I believe God is far more interested in finding passionate people who desire His life and love than He is in cultivating precise people who stop after describing His being and their beliefs.

A Passion for Fullness

HIS PROMISES ARE SURE

*[The promise] is of faith that it might be
according to grace, so that the promise might be sure to
all the seed . . . who are of the . . . faith of Abraham.*

ROMANS 4:16

Do you see how dynamic the guarantees
are in this verse? It shows *hope* where things are as
dead or barren as Abraham's late-in-life
impotency or Sarah's change-of-life womb. It
shows *promise* where "things do not exist," things
that you and I may see as impossibilities.

Whatever lifelessness or unfruitfulness may
taunt you, whether personally or professionally,
we are called by God to lay hold of His promises.

Pastors of Promise

FORGIVE AND BE FORGIVEN

If you do not forgive men their trespasses,
neither will your Father forgive your trespasses.

MATTHEW 6:15

 The Godhead's order of things is established in words that astonish us with a hard spiritual fact: our being forgiven is contingent upon our forgiveness of others. Our answers *from* God depend upon our wills to answer *to* God.

He refuses to raise a breed of sons and daughters who are unlike Him. He insists that every latent trait of our former heritage, as offspring of Adam's race, be wormed out of us. He won't allow unforgiveness to continue. It's not in His nature, so He confronts it in ours.

Prayer Is Invading the Impossible

BEGIN WITH WORSHIP

Present your bodies a living sacrifice, . . .
and . . . be transformed by the renewing of your mind.

ROMANS 12:1

Present your body, daily and literally, to the Lord in worship. Stand or kneel or lift your hands, not as a ritual performance but as a demonstration of praise. In some way each day, present your body in praise to Him. You will find this to be more than a set of calisthenics. Your mind will begin to function differently, for our mind turns toward what our body is given to.

So begin with worship. Before anything else occurs in a day, bow to your knees and say, "Lord, this day is Yours, and so am I." Declare His authority over all your life for all this day.

Glory on Your House

SOMEONE WHO UNDERSTANDS

This High Priest of ours understands our weaknesses.

HEBREWS 4:15, TLB

 We all need someone who understands our feelings, our vulnerability to both emotional and physical pain. We need someone who identifies with the utter weakness of our flesh, especially before the ferocious onslaught of fear, doubt, anger, and lust—temptations that tear at the heart and rip out hope.

Into this need for understanding Jesus comes, above all wanting us to know that He does understand. His suffering has made Him the One to whom we can turn for understanding. *The Visitor*

THE ULTIMATE CROSSROADS

As by one man's disobedience many were
made sinners, so also by one Man's obedience
many will be made righteous.

ROMANS 5:19

The word *crossroads* indicates a point of decision, a point where the future is determined. At Calvary we come to the ultimate crossroads. There we face the most staggering realities this world has ever known:

God's Son died on the Cross,

Man's sin was judged in the Cross,

God's justice was satisfied at the Cross.

What a person does in the face of Calvary's realities determines every aspect of life—here and hereafter.

The Visitor

ABUNDANT LIVING

*I have come that they may have life,
and that they may have it more abundantly.*

JOHN 10:10

 God not only wants to save our souls, He wants to help us make life *work*. He has come to enable us to "reign in life" (Rom. 5:17). That's what He means when He says He has come that we might have life "more abundantly." He is seeking to direct us in a life that functions effectively in everything, at every time, and in every place.

His objective is *release*—to release our living to its maximum potential by calling forth our giving to its fullest possibilities.

The Key to Everything

RECONCILIATION

God . . . has given us the ministry of reconciliation.

2 CORINTHIANS 5:18

The only way to reconcile a broken relationship is for one person to initiate the restoration by trying to understand the other person's fears, past, and pain. None of us is inclined to accept that responsibility, so we need to develop a special openness of heart. We need to refuse the temptation to argue our own case and see beyond the deception that our perception of the situation must be right.

Coming before the Lord with an open heart helps us overcome the temptations of self-defensiveness and insensitivity to others, and will help prevent bitterness or resentment from finding a harbor in our hearts.

Our Daily Walk

THE WEIGHT OF GOD'S GLORY

I will glorify the house of My glory, . . .
I will make the place of My feet glorious.

ISAIAH 60:7, 13

Isaiah declares God's readiness to pour the weight of His worth and working into our lives. As He does, people will be changed. The emptiness and neediness in all of us cry out for His glory.

The weight of God's glory is the only *worth* that can bring true self-worth.

The weight of God's glory is the only *wealth* that can bring true abundance.

The weight of God's glory is the only *force* that can tip the scales and turn the tide of human circumstance from emptiness to fulfillment.

Glory on Your House

GOD-GIVEN OPPORTUNITIES

With God all things are possible.

MATTHEW 19:26

Opportunity is never a matter of pressure with God.

When God opens a door it stays open long enough for us to enter decisively and wisely. His Spirit brings peace to every action, movement, choice, or change that is ordered by Him. The way we abide under the government of His given opportunities is by giving time to prayer.

Bring every opportunity to God, ask His will, wait on Him, and be honest in acknowledging any inner disturbance that may signal His Spirit's cautioning. His doors of opportunity always stay open to His will.

Taking Hold of Tomorrow

WE CRY FOR GOD

The Son of God has come and has given us an
understanding, that we may know Him who is true.

1 JOHN 5:20

 When you're in the middle of a bad day . . .
aim your hard questions at God, not man.

Why? Because in life's darkest hours, there are
usually no human beings with adequate answers.
Counselors may analyze, associates may sympathize,
and experienced friends may empathize. But finite
minds and feeble flesh can never satisfy us with the
Presence we seek, for we truly cry for God Himself,
not answers.

How to Live Through a Bad Day

GOD IS ALWAYS AWAKE

He who keeps Israel shall neither slumber nor sleep.

PSALM 121:4

How clear the Scriptures are that God is always awake and alert, tending to our need: "He who keeps Israel shall neither slumber nor sleep," and "I lay down and slept; I awoke, for the LORD sustained me" (Ps. 3:5). Even while we are at rest, our Father's program for our blessing is being sustained. As surely as your heart is kept beating through the night, His heart concern for you is being carried out.

Whatever the apparent darkness, God never forsakes the works of His hands (see Ps. 138:8).

Dark times are intended for your rest. When they come, lean back and recline in the everlasting arms of God.

Rebuilding the Real You

The Dilemma of Decisions

If any of you lacks wisdom, let him ask
of God, who gives to all liberally and without
reproach, and it will be given to him.

JAMES 1:5

When we are considering any major change or decision in our lives, we must make certain that our "sensible," "practical" plans have first been laid at God's feet. If He is really Lord—the supreme authority of our lives—He must be given veto power over *all* our designs and schemes. Once granted, the dilemma of decision-making is resolved.

Scripture tells us clearly that when famines—*dry times*—come into our lives, the Lord will make it His business to care for those who *rest* their hope in Him rather than *rush* to figure out their own solutions.

A New Time and Place

THE IMPRINT OF HIS NAME

Your kingdom come. Your will be done.

MATTHEW 6:10

To pray "your kingdom come" in all we do is to declare God's imprint in every part of our day. It is to proclaim Christ's lordship over family, work, relationships, and even future plans and goals. It is to ask the Lord to mark every moment with the imprint of Jesus' name.

God desires to stamp our petitions with the imprint of His Son's reality. He longs to impress the mark of Christ's nature and character into everything we do.

Living and Praying in Jesus' Name

Expect Great Things!

*He will be great, and will
be called the Son of the Highest.*

LUKE 1:32

We have a GREAT Savior!

Therefore . . . we are possessors of a great salvation, which encompasses every dimension of human need and deserves to be broadcast to every place where people hurt.

Therefore . . . we are encouraged to expect great victories, knowing that great battles are necessary for conquest, but confident because our Great Savior is leading us.

There is nothing too great for us to expect since we have so great a Savior and Lord.

Moments with Majesty

AVAILABLE TO RENEWAL

*You are complete in Him, who is
the head of all principality and power.*

COLOSSIANS 2:10

Jesus' discipling program requires a constant willingness to be correctable, teachable, and shapeable:

Correctable, because I heed the Spirit's admonishing.

Teachable, because I choose never to presume I know anything so well that there isn't something new I might understand or perceive more clearly.

Shapeable, because I refuse to suppose I have "arrived"—or for that matter, that I ever will!

However much we learn, advance, or progress, we are well-served by a mind-set that keeps available to renewal.

The Power and Blessing

WORTH EVERYTHING

*"Father, I have sinned against heaven and
before you."... His father saw him and had compassion.*

LUKE 15:18, 20

The story of the Prodigal Son is one of
Jesus' most magnificent (Luke 15:11–32). Here is
God's heart completely unveiled. He reaches out
to the most unjustifiably rebellious and miserable
failure. After reading that story of consummate
waste and ruined potential, *now* ask the question:
How does God—Father, Son, and Holy Spirit—
feel about me, my failures, my needs, and my
waste of divinely-provided opportunities?

Jesus' teaching gives an unmistakable answer:
You're worth everything to Him! Your failures
have not removed your possibilities! He welcomes
you with compassion.

Rebuilding the Real You

FEED ON LIVING BREAD

I am weary with my crying; my throat
is dry; my eyes fail while I wait for my God.

PSALM 69:3

There is no weariness like the soul-weariness the psalmist speaks of here. Quick surges of faith may occur in an inspirational moment, but how do you sustain faith during prolonged sickness, continued temptation, or seemingly unending relational struggles?

Feed on living bread. Jesus said, "Man shall not live by bread alone, but by every word that proceeds from the mouth of God" (Matt. 4:4). When you come to the end of yet another day that has drained your physical, emotional, and spiritual strength, sit down and read the Word of God. If you can't stay awake, stand up and read it aloud.

You may not remember brilliant flashes of insight, but your soul is being fed by the Holy Spirit.

The Heart of Praise

A LOVING GOD

When you pray say, "Our Father in heaven."

LUKE 11:2

 With these words Jesus stressed the nature of the Almighty One. We are not approaching a gold-hearted deity or an unpredictable superhuman. What Jesus wants us to grasp in speaking these words is often limited by the relationship we have known with an earthly parent. But God cannot be mirrored in the image of any human being except His Son.

We are coming to a living God who is a loving God. And He loves you!

Prayer Is Invading the Impossible

EARS TO HEAR

Faith comes by hearing,
and hearing by the word of God.

ROMANS 10:17

God's Word has been given to increase growth, fruitfulness, and blessing, both in and through your life. And it is only as you and I keep open to it—keep *listening* with a ready heart to be taught and to obey—that fruit will appear and increase.

Every time the words "He who has ears to hear, let him hear" occur in the New Testament, Jesus is the one who is speaking. This is no casual expression. It is the divine Son of God saying, "Don't ever close your ears or your heart to your need to be taught. It's the key to growth, to fruitfulness, and to the joy of a multiplied harvest of God's blessing in your life."

His is the power. Ours may be the blessing. But how we listen will determine it all.

The Power and Blessing

GOD'S KINGDOM FIRST

*Seek first the kingdom of God and His
righteousness, and all these things shall be added to you.*

MATTHEW 6:33

John Wesley said, "God will do nothing on earth except in answer to believing prayer." In honor of His own Son, whose death made possible the full invasion of divine power into the impossibilities of earth, God will do nothing apart from the prayers of the people His Son redeemed. The power is His; the privilege is ours.

We who are in Christ have no reason to fear or surrender to hell's program. We have been redeemed to be prayerful agents of God's blessing, authority, and power on earth; to pray for the earthly manifestation of His heavenly righteousness and will.

That will happen when we seek God's kingdom first.

Prayer Is Invading the Impossible

PRAY NOW

Men always ought to pray and not lose heart.

LUKE 18:1

Why do we get so busy at everything other than prayer? Why do we say so often, "Well, I've prayed, but what can I do?"

Answer:

Begin to pray and praise immediately when challenging situations arise. Start now.

Speak to Jesus about each matter that begins to trouble you. Don't wait.

Cease from the exhausting toil of carrying worries and cares on your shoulders. Release them.

Seize every opportunity to pray with and for people.

Get alone with the Savior—in the Word and in prayer.

Moments with Majesty

March

I AM . . . LEARNING

TO UNDERSTAND

GOD'S HEART,

TRUSTING IN THE

CERTAINTY OF

HIS WORD.

PRAYER IS ALIVE

The eyes of the LORD are on
the righteous, and His ears are open to their prayers.

1 PETER 3:12

 There is a time to be silent. There is a time to be still, to know the awesomeness of God's person and presence.

But prayer is alive.

It is aloud with praise,

aglow with warmth,

attuned with song,

aflame with power.

And it is also unsettling in its violence.

Not in the violence of its practice, but in the violence of its impact.

Prayer Is Invading the Impossible

AN INNER CORE OF GOD

Create in me a clean heart,
O God, and renew a steadfast spirit within me.

PSALM 51:10

Do fears surround you? Do lusts clamor for attention, eroding your inner integrity? Does anger fester, embittering your attitude toward others? Has unforgiveness lodged deep within, hindering the kind of spiritual growth you'd like to have?

Oh, how these mental and emotional forces work against our will! They cripple our confidence, hinder our attempts to move ahead, and weaken our resistance.

Yet, amid all this and deeper still, remember there is an inner core of God—established hope— for your redeemed spirit! Let that love, peace, and joy abide and secure your heart.

Rebuilding the Real You

SACRIFICIAL LAMB

For the joy that was set before Him,
[He] endured the cross, despising the shame.

HEBREWS 12:2

The power of one emotion overthrew the other—joy overcame shame.

Calvary was a reasoned, predetermined plan in the Father's counsels, and agreed to before all worlds by the Son, who knew He would become the sacrificial Lamb. In intellectual terms, it was all settled. But at Gethsemane, passion rises and blood-sweat oozes from the pores of the God-man who is caught in the emotion and tension of actualizing the redemptive plan.

Indeed, there is a beauty and balance to the whole of His Word and His way, but it can only be realized with passion.

A Passion for Fullness

DAILY MATTERS

Give us this day our daily bread.

MATTHEW 6:11

 God is concerned for daily detail, and we should ask about it.

The most important thing about this is not the discovery that we can ask for God's help in the mundane matters of our personal lives. The most important thing is that we are told to do so. The message is plain. We must ask about day-to-day matters as well as large eternal issues.

Full understanding in prayer leads us to consult the Father about the smallest matters in life, . . . which, in fact, inevitably become the largest if neglected in prayer.

Prayer Is Invading the Impossible

GOD SEEKS WORSHIPPERS

God is Spirit, and those who
worship Him must worship in spirit and truth.

JOHN 4:24

 The Father is seeking people whose worship is spiritually alive and true-hearted" (author's paraphrase of John 4:24). He is seeking worshippers, so we can be assured that if we will worship Him, He will show up!

Worship invites and gives place for the glory of the Lord to be realized and to bless at a given place. It is an act of God's sovereign choice and grace, but it is not arbitrary, random, or accidental. It is a decisive action He promises in response to genuine human hunger for Him.

Glory on Your House

MARCH 6

OPPORTUNITY AND OBEDIENCE

Give me understanding, and I shall live.

PSALM 119:144

People can make serious mistakes by walking through the open doors of an apparent opportunity without consulting the Lord. Sometimes we presume that since we have taken some steps with God's blessing, all our steps will receive the same blessing.

Israel's early victories in Canaan under Joshua's leadership were won with God's direction, but they became an occasion of deception for the men of Gibeon, who forged a treaty with Israel under false pretenses (Joshua 9).

Yesterday's wisdom doesn't insure that we won't walk in foolishness today. We must open our hearts to receive God's teaching and corrections each and every day.

Our Daily Walk

FORGIVING ONE ANOTHER

Be kind to one another, tenderhearted,
forgiving one another, even as God in Christ forgave you.

EPHESIANS 4:32

People who don't forgive tend to be sick. This doesn't mean that all sick people are unforgiving. What it does mean is that many human afflictions are directly traceable to the long-term impact of bitterness, anger, and resentment on the human body. They're all forms of unforgiveness. Our human bodies and personalities were not created to bear the burden of unforgiveness.

Peace of heart, mind, soul, and body can only be enjoyed when God's forgiveness is transmitted *through* us as fully as it has been given *to* us.

The Key to Everything

HONESTY IN PRAYER

Let my prayer come before You;
incline Your ear to my cry.

PSALM 88:2

 Most of us don't pray on a regular basis because we're deeply aware that it will cost us something.

More than time.

More than money.

More than faith.

To lay hold of prayer as my own available resource for effective, practical, daily use—as an abiding certainty in an unpredictable world—will cost me one thing.

Honesty.

Prayer Is Invading the Impossible

THE SHEPHERD'S CALL

I am the good shepherd; and I
know My sheep, and am known by My own.

JOHN 10:14

Spring is the season the shepherds call
their sheep to leave the lowlands and begin to
climb the heights. Fresh grass, sprays of flowers,
and blossoming trees beckon upward.

Hear the upward call of the Master;
lift your eyes and you will see
new horizons appear,
and the challenge is clear,
come and climb the heights with me.
Never let your heart be shackled
by affections earthly bound.
follow Christ today
up the narrow way
that leads to higher ground.

Glorious Morning!

FREE FROM SUFFERING

It was fitting . . . to make the captain
of their salvation perfect through sufferings.

HEBREWS 2:10

Why did Jesus Christ endure a lifetime of struggle, loneliness, stress, temptation, pain, and anguish? And why did He die a slow, torturous death of crucifixion, rather than one of instant, painless demise? The answer is that this Lamb is a means of restoration as well as redemption, and His sufferings were an essential part of that mission.

Hebrews 2:10 says that through Christ's sufferings there was a perfecting, that is, a completion of His Saviorhood. That tells us this: The Son of God submitted to a plan that would include a lifetime of the same kind of suffering you and I experience. And this plan would be a means of setting us free from the oppressive power of that suffering.

The Visitor

Come Expectantly

*"Who will roll away the stone
from the door of the tomb for us?"*

MARK 16:3

The stone that had been rolled across the mouth of Jesus' tomb was larger and heavier than three women could possibly manage. For that matter, it may have been more than three brawny men could have tackled.

The women came anyway. They didn't know what would happen. They didn't know who might help. But everything they had learned about Jesus of Nazareth since they had first met Him taught them to come expectantly.

How do you approach a "great stone" in your life? You choose to come with expectation. Hope is a starting place. You choose to open your heart to hope.

Glorious Morning!

A HOLY LARGESS

Judge not, and you shall not be judged.
Condemn not, and you shall not be condemned.

LUKE 6:37

How easily we succumb to judging and condemning. But by letting the truth of God's Word and the presence of Jesus work in us to stretch the fabric of our souls, a largeness of life will open. First it will open up *in* us, then its bounty can open out *through* us.

So many things change when we grow in the true spirit of giving, that is, in the "spirit of God's release." The bitterness of criticism, the pettiness of judging, the quickness to condemn, and the slowness to forgive—all can be crowded out by a holy largess of loving and giving.

The Key to Everything

HE IS ALIVE!

He is not here; for He is risen, as He said.

MATTHEW 28:6

The disciples, whose dreams of earthly Messianic glory were shattered at the bloody Cross on Mount Calvary, would never—could never—have pulled off a high-minded religious charade.

They would never have regrouped . . . after running in fear for their very lives.

They would never have believed . . . after watching their first ideas of Jesus' purpose and mission explode into a million pieces.

They would never have boldly preached the gospel of His life, death, and resurrection.

They would never have laid down their very lives—as witness to His reality—unless . . . UNLESS . . . *Jesus Christ was alive, and they knew it!*

Glorious Morning!

DAILY CONFESSION

If we confess our sins to him, he can be depended
on to forgive us and to cleanse us from every wrong.

1 JOHN 1:9, TLB

We must offer daily confession, both for known sins that blot a day's activities and for sins we may have overlooked.

When we do this, we are assured that through the blood of Christ we have instant and complete forgiveness.

Every aspect of our lives, regardless of what the world says is right or acceptable, needs to be brought under the searching eyes of the Lord.

Our Daily Walk

CONFIDANT OF THE CREATOR

The LORD confides in those who fear him.

PSALM 25:14, NIV

Imagine being the confidant of the Creator and Sustainer of the universe, in whom lie all of life's secrets! Think of being able to know the will of Him who "does great things which we cannot comprehend" (Job 37:5).

The primary part of God's master plan for the ages is an open book to those who enter into covenant with Him, for that plan is Jesus! You don't have to be initiated into a secret society to relate to the God of the Bible. The Christian life is not mystical or magical; it is lived and expressed in the Light.

The Heart of Praise

LIGHT OF HIS LOVE

Since we, God's children, are human beings—
made of flesh and blood—he became flesh and blood, too.

HEBREWS 2:14, TLB

The significance of the Cross is that the Son of God died there: the only-begotten offspring of the Almighty One of heaven. He is unique. No one like Him has been born before or since. He is specifically, and especially, the Savior sent from above. At the Cross He fulfilled His purpose in coming. He who came to share the experience of life *with* us, submitted to death *for* us.

He loves us with an everlasting love. We can place our every problem at the foot of the Cross and let the light of His everlasting love and almighty triumph shine on it.

The Visitor

COMMITTED TO YOUR SUCCESS

*Oh, the depth of the riches both of the wisdom
and knowledge of God! How unsearchable are His
judgments and His ways past finding out!*

ROMANS 11:33

Have you ever hesitated to obey or surrender to God's will on this unspoken-but-felt suspicion, "If I let God take full control of my life, He'll deny my dreams and block my goals?"

Dear friend, God is totally *committed* to your success. He also has sufficient wisdom and power to see you brought to your fullest potential. He is *El Shaddai*—the Lord God Sufficient-and-Almighty, our living, loving God! He's the God of true opportunities, not lost ones.

Taking Hold of Tomorrow

HONEST BEFORE GOD

*If we confess our sins, He is faithful
and just to forgive us our sins and to cleanse us
from all unrighteousness.*

1 JOHN 1:9

 The Greek word for "confess" is *homologeo.*
It means, "to speak the same thing." That is, to say
about sin what God is saying to you about it.

Confession involves being honest, forthright,
and not excusing yourself either to God or to your
own conscience.

If the Father says, "I don't want you to do that,"
then respond, "Lord, I don't want to do that."

Rebuilding the Real You

OUR SINLESS SUBSTITUTE

He Himself is the propitiation for our sins.

1 JOHN 2:2

Many people think it's necessary to negotiate with God in order to be accepted by Him. They pray, "Lord, I'll do this for You if You'll do that for me." But Christ has done everything necessary to fulfill any vow we could make to "better ourselves" in God's eyes. On these terms we can come to God freely, knowing we are forgiven fully. What a joyous reality!

As our sinless substitute before God, Jesus poured out His life on the Cross. Since Jesus is absolutely perfect, God sees the record of His sinless life instead of our sin and accepts us *completely*.

Living and Praying in Jesus' Name

THE POWER IS HIS

In Your hand is power and might.

1 CHRONICLES 29:12

The sovereign God of the universe has committed Himself to write the history of earth. But He has willed to do it through people, and He invites you and me to respond with chapters of bold accomplishments done in His name.

You probably feel as I do when such an enormous truth dawns upon you. "What can I do? It's too much for me."

But wait. Remember, the power is HIS! He is the Publisher. He's simply looking for writers. For people who will trust the power of His Holy Spirit to work in the common, ordinary affairs of their daily lives—family, business, relationships, schoolwork, difficulties, ministry opportunities.

God offers a blank book of possibilities and asks what we are going to write.

Moments with Majesty

Changed from the Inside

*Do not be conformed to this world,
but be transformed by the renewing of your mind.*

ROMANS 12:2

 People think they can scratch their inner itches by changing their image . . . changing their wardrobes . . . changing their cars . . . changing their careers . . . or even changing their wives or husbands.

But the Word of God warns us against looking for inner peace and satisfaction by making external changes!

Only the Lord can bring about true change or genuine fulfillment, and He does it from the inside out. He alone can satisfy a restless heart.

A New Time and Place

PATHWAY OF TRIUMPH

*I have been crucified with Christ; it is
no longer I who live, but Christ lives in me.*

GALATIANS 2:20

Listen carefully, please. The path of the
Cross is not to be mistaken or misunderstood.

It *isn't* intended as a habit of commiserating
over life's tough stuff, while muttering, "I guess it's
just my cross."

It *isn't* a life of religious self-denial, pretending
that a prudish, self-styled piety is what God calls for.

It *isn't* a dour pathway that touts suffering
and defeat as the ultimate expression of true
holiness! Never!

The Cross is the pathway of surrender and of
refusal to be dominated by selfishness or carnality.
But beyond it all, at the bottom line, the Cross is
a pathway of *triumph!*

The Power and Blessing

SOURCE OF EVERYTHING

Abide in Me, and I in you.
As the branch cannot bear fruit of itself.

JOHN 15:4

Abide in Me," . . . Christ has said.

It's so simple. So clear.

First and foremost, Jesus wants us to experience, sustain, and enjoy a personal, intimate walk with Him.

It isn't that He's disinterested in the demands of our daily duties or the pressures of our private world. Far from it. He just knows that the fountainhead of life is with Him. He is the Source—of everything.

Strength for your day. Wisdom for your task. Comfort for your soul. Grace for your battle. Provision for each need. Understanding for each failure.

Everything!

Moments with Majesty

"Let It Be You"

*Your kingdom come. Your will
be done, on earth as it is in heaven.*

LUKE 11:2

The God we worship is the Lord of creation, and His power knows no limits except those He imposes on Himself. Here is one of them: He waits to work His will on earth in answer to humans who ask. His kingdom—His eternal rulership—will only rule on earth where it is invited.

It is not a question of His ability to dominate on the sheer strength of His own intent. But with reference to earth and people He has chosen to confine Himself to specific channels of operation. He wills to work through people. Rebels may resist, sin may abound, but He will find someone through whom He can work.

Jesus is saying, "Let it be you."

Prayer Is Invading the Impossible

DESIGN AND DISCIPLINE

If we hope for what we do not see,
we eagerly wait for it with perseverance.

ROMANS 8:25

Dreams and visions—God's heaven-born designs for life—are promised to the Spirit-filled saint. Without them, serving God becomes hit-or-miss. But we need to observe disciplines that are clearly enunciated in His Word. Without designs *and* disciplines, we become either visionaries who gain dreams from God yet aimlessly chase them, or legalists who know biblical guidelines but live them antiseptically, out of touch with the life-giving Spirit who gave them.

The divinely targeted life seeks the *way* of the Lord revealed by the Spirit in prayer and obeys the *will* of the Lord as revealed in His Word.

The Leading Edge

Prevailing Prayer

*Whatever you bind on earth will be
bound in heaven, and whatever you loose on earth
will be loosed in heaven.*

MATTHEW 16:19

 Prayers are pleas for God's ordained order
to appear.

Prayers prevail above earth-powers.

Prayers overthrow hell-powers.

In this verse we are told by our Lord,
"Whenever you determine to lay claim to the
Father's counsels as opposed to the adversary's,
you'll find that earth can have what heaven has
already decided on!"

Prayer Is Invading the Impossible

No Struggle Is Pointless

It is finished!

JOHN 19:30

 The dawn of world redemption had broken, and with it the chains of human slavery to sin, shame, and condemnation were being shattered.

"It is finished!" was the Son of God's invitation to join Him in the conviction that now—because of the Cross—there is nothing we struggle with that is without either a purpose or an end. No struggle need ever be pointless. No suffering need ever be unending.

How to Live Through a Bad Day

ADORATION AND DEVOTION

Pray without ceasing.

1 THESSALONIANS 5:17

In giving a series of concise commands for disciples, the aged apostle wrote, *"Pray without ceasing."*

Whatever else may be said about either *living* as a disciple of Jesus Christ or *walking* with Him in faith, prayer is the one discipline above and beneath all others.

It is a combination of

worship—through adoration, praise, and thanksgiving *to* God,

fellowship—through devotion, communion, and conversation *with* God,

intercession—through supplication, fasting, and spiritual warfare *before* God.

The Power and Blessing

LEARNING TO PRAY

He departed to the mountain to pray.

MARK 6:46

 Disciples of Jesus are prayer-learners. We learn to pray *in* prayer and *by* prayer.

I *hear* Jesus teaching prayer, and it prompts me to action:

He taught solitude in prayer (Matt. 6:6)

He taught humility and tenacity in prayer (Luke 11:1–13)

He taught faithfulness in prayer (Luke 18:1)

He taught power in prayer (Mark 11:22–26)

I *see* Jesus at prayer, and it moves me:

When He had sent them away, He departed to the mountain to pray (Mark 6:46).

Moments with Majesty

WORDS ARE POWERFUL

With the heart one believes unto righteousness,
and with the mouth confession is made unto salvation.

ROMANS 10:10

When the odds are stacked against you and you've chosen the course of trusting God, just keep walking—don't talk about it. Words are powerful . . . to weaken as well as to build up. Words spoken unadvisedly or lightly can compromise our commitment by our either *under*stating God's promise because of our fears, or by our *over*stating our faith because we don't want to appear foolish.

Walking in the spirit of trust means simply doing what the Holy Spirit directs you to do. And keeping quiet.

Taking Hold of Tomorrow

BE HOLY

As He who called you is holy,
you also be holy in all your conduct.

1 PETER 3:15

Be it stage, screen, television, or video, each of us must beware the incipient darkness that seeks to dim our light and dull our focus. I have to keep free from the soul-wasting effect of the godless giddiness I encounter while seeking to enjoy simple comedy. I must avoid the abounding sexual innuendo present in virtually all dramas today. I need to keep myself from the profuse profanity, blatant blasphemy, and sensitivity-numbing violence that are included in the price tag of a brief excursion into an adventure flick.

Simply put, to function with spiritual authority requires that I live in purity.

The Leading Edge

April

JESUS,

MASTER

OF THE TUMULT,

YOU WHO CALMED

THE TROUBLED SEA;

WEARY I REPAIR

TO THEE.

CLOTHED IN HIS GLORY

Christ in you, the hope of glory

COLOSSIANS 1:27

Created to know the presence of God's glory, we yearn for its reality while little understanding the path to its recovery. We need not only forgiveness for sin but the fulfillment sin deprives us of.

As Adam and Eve snatched leaves to cover themselves, so we still attempt desperately not only to cover our naked sinfulness before God, but to substitute something for the loss of being clothed in His glory. The splendor of God's presence was essentially what Adam and Eve wore before the Fall. Thus, the first couple's sudden awareness had less to do with their nudity than with their sense that God's glory had departed.

The only goal that will fully grant the desire for substance to our lives is to become clothed again in the glory of God.

Glory on Your House

GOD IS OUR REWARD

I am your . . . exceedingly great reward.

GENESIS 15:1

God never demands a sacrifice for the divine pleasure of smelling its aroma or because He needs us to tickle His pride. The objective is *our* release—*our* growth.

God asked Abraham to offer Isaac. Not to exploit Abraham's emotions or to destroy Isaac, but to take away forever Abraham's fear that God might not have his best interest at heart. Only in worship do we draw close enough to discern God's true nature and loving heart.

God gave Abraham no immediate monetary reward for worshiping Him, but the reward was immensely grander—God Himself!

Heart of Praise

PURSUING GOD'S WAY

*There is therefore now no
condemnation to those who are in Christ Jesus.*

ROMANS 8:1

That verse deserves a loud *"Hallelujah!"* because this is the bright truth about our new God-given inheritance! But of equal certainty is the continuing presence of personal problems bequeathed to us from our pasts—things that impact our lives with drastic consequence.

YES! Our salvation does solve the problem of our relationship with God. NO! It doesn't dissolve all the problems in our lives. New life in Christ opens the doorway to solutions but only by walking through that door and patiently pursuing God's way will those problems finally reach *resolution.*

Rebuilding the Real You

INVADING THE IMPOSSIBLE

Lord, teach us to pray.

LUKE 11:1

Jesus' disciples asked Him, "Lord, teach us to pray."

In response, Jesus taught them nothing of mysticism, religious pretense, or meditation. Nothing of bizarre physical contortions or memorized incantations attended by clouds of incense.

But He did teach them something about violence. Jesus was very clear about it: Prayer is a matter of war—prayer is about invasion, assault, and force.

On earth-side, things may seem impenetrable, yet from the heaven-side, activated by prayer, there is a spiritual violence that can invade and overthrow the impossible.

Prayer Is Invading the Impossible

GOD'S FAITHFULNESS

Then Isaac sowed . . . reaped . . . and the
LORD blessed Him . . . until he became very prosperous.

GENESIS 26:12–13

Blessing is always the beginning place of
divine commission.

God never calls us to action or service without
first having established grounds from which we may
move. That is the sovereign side of all the issues of
life. He gives first and He gives most. Whatever we
are asked to respond with is always "afterward and
less than," for He summons our faith *after* He has
displayed His faithfulness.

A Passion for Fullness

COME TO THE CROSS

"Truly this was the Son of God!"

MATTHEW 27:54

I find such comfort clinging to the unshakable truths of Easter—truths that cannot be altered, diminished, or diluted by the passage of time or human follies and frailties.

God's Word is TRUE.

Christ's Cross is SUFFICIENT TO SAVE.

JESUS IS LORD.

Let us come to His Cross again, unmistakably assured in the salvation it affords, and unswerving in our commitment to Him.

In a world where no piece of ground seems secure, this is our sure and unshakable Rock.

Glorious Morning!

HAPPY HOLINESS

Oh, worship the LORD in the beauty of holiness!

PSALM 96:9

When the Holy Spirit fills a life or a house, let's not expect Him to neutralize the true humanity God created. He can work in true "holiness" the restoration of God's original, pre-sin-tainted plan for human beings. The Holy Spirit's indwelling human flesh will not produce a hybrid—something neither completely divine nor completely human. Instead, His presence in our lives, as in our homes, will bring about a thoroughly spiritual and genuinely natural person—people who are holy in their happiness with happy expressions of holiness.

Look at Jesus! He is the evidence that holiness and humanity can be blended successfully, beautifully, and without affectation.

Glory on Your House

KING OF GLORY

Who is this King of Glory?
The LORD of hosts, He is the King of glory.

PSALM 24:10

Christ's return to heaven is as sudden as His departure. The angelic hosts anticipate the joyful reunion with the Beloved One. But upon rising at the Eternal Father's command, their voices and instruments set for a welcoming fanfare, they are stunned. They hadn't expected Him to return as a man. Perhaps He would sojourn as one, but to be a man for eternity? They had sacrificed heaven's dearest treasure in sending Him, and now the return on their investment is a glorious—but wounded—man! And as this man strides towards them, you can almost hear them ask, "Is this the Son . . . ?"

Then an assuring crescendo rises from the throne: "This is He, the King of Glory!"

The Visitor

SAVIOR OF THE WORLD

Go therefore and make disciples of all the nations.

MATTHEW 28:19

Make no mistake, the apostles were tough-minded men. A mixture of hard-working, clear-thinking guys who came to their conclusions independent of one another. There were no "soft sells" in the bunch, and yet all of them, having seen and spent time with the resurrected Lord, set the course of their lives to declare the triple truth:

Jesus of Nazareth is the Messiah.

Jesus is the Son of God, Savior of the World.

Jesus' resurrection proves the above is true.

Glorious Morning!

POWER AND PARTNERSHIP

The generous soul will be made rich,
and he who waters will also be watered himself.

PROVERBS 11:25

God promises "all power" available for "all possibilities"—His power and our partnership.

Think of it! God promises that when we open the faucet of possibility through our own giving, a heavenly reservoir is waiting to flow toward us with a whole lot more than you or I could ever contain. But we decide how open the faucet will be, and thereby determine how much of His divine flow will move in our direction.

The Key to Everything

CALLED TO HOLINESS

Be holy, for I am holy.

1 PETER 1:16

God's purpose in calling us to purity—in teaching us to examine our hearts, bare our souls, confess our sins, and receive His cleansing—must always be kept in view. God does not seek holiness for holiness's sake. He's not in the business of making people clean so He can put them on pedestals like plaster images. Instead, He calls us to holiness for an entirely practical reason. The goal of a day-by-day quest for a perfect heart, wise actions, and sensitive speech is to make every day of our lives worthwhile.

Our Daily Walk

"Good" Friday

This Man, after He had offered one sacrifice
for sins forever, sat down at the right hand of God.

HEBREWS 10:12

There are reasons Good Friday is called "good," but they are not related to our usual human notions of nice, happy, or comfortable. Rather, the "good" in that day is that it is the day God's love gift of His Son, who arrived in Bethlehem years before, surrendered to death on a Cross in Jerusalem.

The "good" is in the Good Shepherd, laying His life down for His sheep.

The "good" is in the fact that, at the price of Jesus' lifeblood, forgiveness for my sin and yours is now an abiding provision with eternal hope and promise.

How to Live Through a Bad Day

PRAISE AND WORSHIP

Worship Him who made heaven and earth.

REVELATION 14:7

Let us worship with a regenerated spirit, connecting the eternal part of our beings with the Eternal Spirit of God.

Let us worship with a renewed mind, seeking to know as fully as we can the God whom we worship.

Let us praise God with revived emotions, not allowing pseudo-sophistication to make us too embarrassed for passionate praise.

And let us not be afraid to worship God with a rededicated body—placed, as it were, on the altar of sacrifice.

The Heart of Praise

WAIT FOR GOD'S WAY

God . . . does great things which we cannot comprehend.

JOB 37:5

The whole mindset of our culture is to stretch beyond what we think we can do. How many of us, without first seeking God's will, have jumped into situations, seized opportunities, and then found ourselves struggling financially, mentally, or emotionally?

Later, we realized that if we had waited on God we could have discovered His better way.

May we learn to live in that quiet, "waiting" mode in which the Holy Spirit works and directs our hearts. We choose to wait on God to manage our tomorrows rather than maneuvering them ourselves. Tasting tomorrow's promise doesn't require any maneuvering on our part. The promise is fulfilled for those who learn to wait.

Taking Hold of Tomorrow

SEALED AND DELIVERED

Not My will, but Yours, be done.

LUKE 22:42

Consider with me. If Jesus could have called for angels to spare Him the suffering of the Cross (Matt. 26:53), don't you know that He could have called for an early deliverance from death? The message of His submission to the Father's timing as well as the Father's plan is profound in its application to your life and mine.

Have you entrusted everything concerning your case to Jesus? If you have, then the entire matter is sealed and delivered . . . in His resurrection.

Glorious Morning!

THE GRANDEST GRACE

*All have sinned and fall short of the glory
of God, being justified freely by His grace through
the redemption that is in Christ Jesus.*

ROMANS 3:23–24

The instant you received Jesus as your Savior, you entered a new standing with God. The Epistle to the Romans repeatedly uses the word *justified* to describe this action. It's a giant of a concept—a word meaning that God, the Judge of all mankind, has made a legal judgment about you and me. When we trust in Christ, He not only declares us holy, He also gives His legal reasons for doing so. Because we are putting our trust in the righteousness of Christ instead of our own achievement, God puts the sinless record of His Son as a credit to our account.

He not only removes the record of our guilt, He enters the record of Christ's absolute sinlessness! It's astounding and amazing!

Rebuilding the Real You

LIFE AND POWER

*If the same Spirit that raised Christ from the
dead dwells in your body, He will bring God's life and
power into every part of your present experience.*

ROMANS 8:11 (AUTHOR'S PARAPHRASE)

It wasn't an earthquake that rolled the massive stone from the doorway of the tomb. It was an angel. And it wasn't to let Jesus out, because He had already vacated the premises! The Resurrection was already history, and the mighty angel threw open that door to show an empty tomb.

And that empty tomb boldly declares that if death has been conquered, there is *nothing* that can ultimately defeat you. Whatever would press in upon you, whatever insistent voices might whisper words of doubt and despair in your ear, you may take your stand at the open door. With an empty tomb behind you, you may say with confidence, "By the resurrection power of Jesus Christ, nothing can ever defeat me!"

Glorious Morning!

HONEST HEARTS

It is God . . . who has shown in our hearts
to give the light of the knowledge of the glory of God.

2 CORINTHIANS 4:6

Are you ready for God to do something new in your life? I believe He desires to help us discern those things that could keep us from finding the new time and place He has for each of us. He seeks honest hearts, open to His call.

Who says you know what's next for your life?

Who says God can't use you in a dramatic, wholly unexpected way?

Who says He can't lead you into a season of life and ministry beyond anything you've ever experienced—or even dreamed?

Just who is the limiting factor here? Is it God? Or are we capable of closing our hearts to what He wants to do in and through our lives?

A New Time and Place

Alpha and Omega

*He who has begun [alpha] a good work in you
will complete it until [omega] the day of Jesus Christ.*

PHILIPPIANS 1:6

Christ, the Alpha and the Omega, is Lord over the very beginnings and endings of our lives. Today is His, completely. Everything that concerns us—from being born to dying—is in His control. For example, Christ is master over the beginning and ending of my work, including all that concerns me about finding, holding, or even losing a job.

Christ, the "author and finisher of our faith" (Heb. 12:2), is the initiator of life's every detail. He originates and creates all we need to start our journey as well as finish it. He not only gives us new life in Him, He completes it.

Living and Praying in Jesus' Name

THE FINALE

It is finished!

JOHN 19:30

Tetelesthai—It is finished!

The most significant single word in the Greek New Testament translates to the most triumphant declaration. It contains both a prophecy and a verdict. Jesus, the Son, prophesied the momentarily impending conclusion of His saving work, and even before the Cross's finale, He anticipated the Father's verdict and His ultimate intervention.

The dawn of the world's redemption had broken, and with it the chains of human slavery to sin, shame, and condemnation were shattered.

How to Live Through a Bad Day

TRIUMPH ON TIME

*Wait on the LORD; be of good
courage, and He shall strengthen your heart.*

PSALM 27:14

I can't number the times I have wished God would hurry up— . . . with an answer to my prayer . . . with a bailout in the middle of my muddle . . . with a fresh sense of His working in my life.

But there is one well-established principle in the Scriptures, and it is dramatically demonstrated in Jesus' experience.

You can't rush a resurrection. As surely as Jesus rose on time, your triumph will be on schedule also.

Glorious Morning!

GOD OUR HEALER

I am the LORD who heals you.

God's statement, *"I am the LORD who heals you,"* reveals more than just the healing aspect of His nature. Whenever God uses the term "I Am" He is calling our attention to His timelessness, His self-completeness, and His absolute love—everything that flows from His being.

God says, "I Am who I Am." He never changes and is still the same today as He was when He revealed Himself with those words to Moses (Exod. 3:14). God is still the same today as He was when He pledged His covenant of healing to the Israelites at the waters of Marah. He is God our Healer today.

Grounds for Living

The Father's Viewpoint

*As the heavens are higher than the earth,
so are My ways higher than your ways, and My
thoughts than your thoughts.*

ISAIAH 55:9

God is a Father who teaches us, "As the heavens are higher than the earth, so are My ways higher than your ways, and My thoughts than your thoughts." In no uncertain terms, He shows us that His viewpoint and wisdom are many rungs higher than ours.

We're foolish unless we always make Him our point of reference for counsel. He has the master plan of our life and, knowing the end from the beginning, is best prepared to lead us.

Trust Him with your destiny. Trials, suffering, or tragedy may often seem the end. Yet one day, after we have walked farther down life's road, we will be able to look back and say, "Oh, Father. I see. Now I see!"

Moments with Majesty

ALWAYS ON TIME

We are His workmanship,
created in Christ Jesus for good works.

EPHESIANS 2:10

Jesus Christ is very direct with His disciples. He never issues a call that we're incapable of responding to, but the timing of His call *always* seems too soon to us. We think we need *more*—more time, more money, more preparations, more qualifications, more . . .

But the Savior is also a saver of time when it involves His purposes. He won't waste it by calling us into His purpose prematurely or by allowing us to linger beyond the timing He knows is best.

The Power and Blessing

WORTHY OF WORSHIP

Because He is your LORD, worship Him.

PSALM 45:11

I was astounded sometime back to learn that our English word *worship* has its root in the word *worth*.

It began to unfold in my understanding. Real worship of God isn't the exercise of a religious ritual. It's the reflection of a proper value judgment formed about God. I most honor the God who created me and the Lord Jesus who redeemed me, when I ascribe the right value to Him.

He's worth our praise, adoration, and exaltation. Let us worship the Father, praise the Son, and be filled with the Spirit.

Moments with Majesty

PROCLAIMING PRAISE

I have proclaimed . . . righteousness in the
great assembly; indeed, I do not restrain my lips.

PSALM 40:9

The joys of private praise are readily matched by the joys of corporate praise. Small wonder the Word encourages us not to forsake "the assembling of ourselves together" (Heb. 10:25).

In the Psalms, repeated references to sharing the things of God "in the great assembly" emphasize the same truth: Worship involves the whole people of God, not just individuals. God's righteousness and love and truth are too momentous to be hidden in the heart. The spirit of praise begs to "go public"! *The Heart of Praise*

CONFESSION AND INTERCESSION

Create in me a clean heart, O God,
and renew a steadfast spirit within me.

PSALM 51:9

The wisest believer is that one who comes openhearted for cleansing, and who knows that God's summons to repentance is *gracious*. Repentance makes way for a progressive alteration of our thinking, attitude, and heart. God invites us to experience His cleansing and forgiveness, but not self-condemnation or death-dealing despair.

In other words, introspection and confession are to release us . . . and that release opens the door for bold, history-shaping, nation-changing intercession.

Moments with Majesty

THREE IN ONE

There are three that bear witness in heaven:
the Father, the Word, and the
Holy Spirit; and these three are one.

1 JOHN 5:7

The Trinity is to be worshipped: "Praise Father, Son, and Holy Ghost," the doxology lauds.

Petitioning the Father acknowledges His right to rule and decide in all matters.

Glorifying Jesus the Savior is exalting Him who died that we might live.

Honoring the Holy Spirit is giving place to His workings in and through our lives.

Prayer Is Invading the Impossible

REDEMPTIVE POSSIBILITIES

I exhort first of all that supplications, prayers, intercessions, and giving of thanks be made for all men.

1 TIMOTHY 2:1

There's no escaping the assignment in that verse—intercede, and do it thankfully!

The biblical call to intercession has never included the promise that we would be put in control of the answers—only that we could be assured of God's entry into the situation.

Intercessory prayer is not to secure our will. Rather, intercession wars against the powers of darkness given reign by human sin and failure. It resists the efforts of hell at mastering multitudes and invites God's dominion over the enemy of our souls. His sovereignty introduces redemptive possibilities.

The Leading Edge

GOD'S MOUTHPIECE

If anyone speaks, let him speak as the oracles of God.

1 PETER 4:11

We who were fathered by the God who spoke all things into existence and who were redeemed by Him who is called the "Word" ought to be aware that what we say is phenomenally powerful.

Among the disciplines Jesus introduces into our lives is a new sense of responsibility for the words that cross the threshold of our lips.

The words of those made alive by God's spirit are shaping forces. They can create, bind up, release . . . or they can destroy.

"If anyone speaks, let him speak as the oracles of God." That essentially means we are God's mouthpiece. You and I must speak like sons and daughters of the Most High.

Moments with Majesty

May

LIFT YOUR HANDS,

EXALT HIM EVER;

JESUS IS ALIVE!

GOD'S RADIANT PRESENCE

The LORD will create above every dwelling place
. . . a cloud and smoke by day
and the shining of a flaming fire by night.

ISAIAH 4:5

To Isaiah's hearers, these words meant far more than a religious experience in a religious place. It promised that the presence of God would bring hope, healing, wholeness, and happiness right where they lived!

The protective covering of the Almighty God was forecast to ensure both the warm flame of His presence to bless His people and the warring power of His wrath to battle against their enemies. The prophet was foretelling the possibility of homes like yours and mine being lighted with the glow of God's love, filled with the brightness of His blessing, and defended by the fire of His fury on any attempts of the adversary.

Glory on Your House

AT THE FEET OF JESUS

Then great multitudes came to Him,
having with them the lame, blind, mute, maimed,
and many others; and they laid
them down at Jesus' feet, and He healed them.

MATTHEW 15:30

There is no night so long or so dark that Jesus cannot see you through if you will come and lay your burdens at His feet. When we learn to wait at the feet of the Lord, He will bring us through the darkness and into the light of a new day.

People may learn how to pray and how to praise. People may come into the assembly of believers and lift their hands and glorify the Lord and sing a thousand songs. Yet these things will never substitute for those long hours at the feet of Jesus. Those who have learned to live at His feet, clinging to His promises and waiting on Him, experience a dimension of life and fruitfulness beyond what they have ever known before.

A New Time and Place

GOD GIVES AND GIVES

Thanks be to God for His indescribable gift!

2 CORINTHIANS 9:15

What God gives us is completely unearned, and the way He gives is from the abounding provision of the Almighty, All-Sufficient One.

From the moment of my entry into the saving life Jesus has given me through the Cross, all the way through my lifetime of learning to walk in His love and power . . . it's all grace. He gives it. Nothing is earned. Nothing is accomplished through my strength or power. As the hymn writer put it, "He giveth, and giveth, and giveth again."

Come . . . and Behold Him!

BE FORGIVING

Love keeps no record of wrongs.

1 CORINTHIANS 13:5, NIV

Virtually every clash in human relationships is due to an unwillingness to give—to for*give* failure or to *give* understanding.

How soon we all forget the greatness of grace that looked beyond our faults and forgave us. How easily we fall prey to hasty judgment. How slow we are to measure the relative failure of those who violate us against the backdrop of our violations against God.

Jesus has come to bring heaven's rule into our hearts. The forgiven are called to be forgiving—to the same degree that we have been entirely, unconditionally, and graciously forgiven!

The Key to Everything

DEPENDING ON GOD

Take your sandals off your feet,
for the place where you stand is holy ground.

EXODUS 3:5

The essence of this command has to do
with more than reverencing God. It calls us to this
understanding: Step out of the working of what
man can make and onto the grounds of what only
God can create!

God's call to take off our shoes is a summons
to us—a call to that same "barefooted" stance of
childlike dependence that Moses and Joshua reveal.
He wants us to remember and reverence these facts:

He who created us is able to deliver us.

He who appoints His purpose in us is able to
accomplish it through us.

Taking Hold of Tomorrow

SERVANT LEADERS

*Whoever desires to become great
among you, let him be your servant.*

MATTHEW 20:26

We are beginning to see—even in some contemporary corporate structures—that the Master was right when He said the most effective leaders are those who will be servants instead of lords. It's Jesus' style, of course, and He's called you and me to learn it. Unlike false views of macho maleness, He holds up the ideal that "whoever desires to become great among you, let him be your servant."

The message: Strong leaders don't have to burn down the town and trample the citizens to display their leadership potential.

Rebuilding the Real You

BUILD IN FAITH

The grace of God that
brings salvation has appeared to all men.

TITUS 2:11

God's sovereign grace besets us before and behind and overspreads and undergirds our lives. We deserve nothing, but we are inheritors of all. We stumble forward, kept all the while by His power and made fruitful in spite of ourselves! Grace is the fountainhead of all we can become. But that lesson learned, it is our wisdom to see that grace has never been shown as an end in itself.

Grace is the footing upon which God calls us to build in faith.

A Passion for Fullness

FILLED WITH SONG

*He appointed those who should sing to
the LORD, and who should praise the beauty of holiness.*

2 CHRONICLES 20:21

Sing at the day's beginning and sing at the end. Sing together around the dinner table as your occasional expression of table grace. Let's fill our houses with the song of the Lord!

Look at the promises that describe the power of song:

Isaiah 54:1—Song creates the environment for new life when barrenness has blocked our fruitfulness.

2 Chronicles 20:21–22—Song declares, "The battle is the Lord's" when trial comes, and song will scatter the adversary's opposition.

Glory on Your House

REST FOR THE WEARY

Come to Me, all you who labor and
are heavy laden, and I will give you rest.

MATTHEW 11:28

Jesus understands weariness. As a small ship crosses Galilee, and a storm's fury terrifies His companions, Jesus sleeps.

His physical frame is worn and His stamina spent from ministering to multitudes. So worn and weary is He that even the crashing of the waves, the whipping of the boat, and the shrieking of the winds do not awaken Him.

If you've ever felt so tired you couldn't take another step, and if you've wondered whether God knew that feeling, here's your answer: There is One who not only knows your weariness but who says, "I'll walk the next step with you because I've been where you are . . . and further."

The Visitor

WINDOWS OF HEAVEN

I will . . . open . . . the windows of heaven
and pour out for you such blessing that there will
not be room enough to receive it.

MALACHI 3:10

The "windows of heaven" aren't a bank, but they are the openings from which all of life's blessings flow.

When the windows of heaven are open over your home, there is joy and happiness.

When the windows of heaven are open over your business, there is fruitfulness and prosperity.

When the windows of heaven are open over your mind, there is peace and confidence.

When the windows of heaven are open over your body and soul, there is health and contentment.

God loves to bless His children.

The Key to Everything

WORKABLE LIVING

So teach us to number our days,
that we may gain a heart of wisdom.

PSALM 90:12

Wisdom is knowing the right thing to do at the right time. That kind of living is the outward goal of seeking holiness. Taking time daily to review our lives at Jesus' feet is the means to wholesome, healthy, fruitful work and relationships. And that's the goal of holiness: well-rounded, fulfilling, workable living.

But God also has an inward purpose for drawing us toward a holy life—that we become like His Son, Jesus, and that the holiness—the wholeness—of His life in us would overflow to others.

Our Daily Walk

REACH FOR IT!

Because Your lovingkindness is better
than life, my lips shall praise You. . . . I will lift up
my hands in Your name.

PSALM 63:3–4

The psalmist speaks of God's lovingkindness being "better than life" in the same breath as his statement about worshiping with uplifted hands. It's not that he doesn't appreciate his temporal life, but in worship he reaches for more of God's dimension of life.

Let us remember that the "gift of eternal life" promised the believer is not just life unending, it is also unlimited. It is life that is eternal in quantity but also eternal in quality since God infuses us with the traits of His lovingkindness. That's worth reaching for!

The Heart of Praise

Two Kingdoms Clashing

Jesus answered, "My kingdom is not of this world."

JOHN 18:36

The Lord Jesus Christ promised to return again. In the interim, we are not merely charged to witness of His Love. We are explicitly commanded to introduce His rulership—the kingdom of God—into those circumstances in which mankind's lost rule has produced impossible situations.

Christ's whole life presents a clear picture of two kingdoms in opposition. That picture may be seen wherever truth confronts the universal Liar, reality exposes the sham of religiosity, health crashes into the domain of sickness, deliverance unshackles spiritual bondage, love overflows fear, forgiveness expels condemnation, and where wholeness expands the constriction caused by sin.

Prayer Is Invading the Impossible

TRUE WORSHIP

True worshipers will worship the Father in spirit
and truth; for the Father is seeking such to worship Him.

JOHN 4:23

The Greek word *proskuneo* (worship) means "to prostrate oneself before God." Humility is at the heart of true worship. This issue focuses not so much on physical prostration as on prostrating our pride before Him.

We need to lay our human wills before Him, to demonstrate childlike humility and obedience through our submission to His way in worship. Any human insistence on "my dignity" is unworthy. It is frothy stuff before the *chabod*, the glory of God!

Let us praise Him! Thank Him! Laud Him! Adore Him!

Glory on Your House

Grace Enters the Scene

Born again, not of corruptible seed but incorruptible,
through the word of God which lives and abides forever.

1 PETER 1:23

Unholy" is more than a stamp of failure
on our faces. It is the word that describes our loss
of the only thing that could produce
completeness in our lives. "But God demonstrates
His . . . love toward us" (Rom. 5:8).

It is here, at the point of our helplessness to
change anything, that God's saving, healing,
freeing love and grace enter the scene. He sends His
Holy Son to die for our sins and redeem us; then
He sends His Holy Spirit to fill our lives and
restore us! He has set forth a holy power to birth us
all over again, then, by this "new birth" to sow into
our human nature a new seed—a new, restoring
genetic principle making possible "wholeness."

Rebuilding the Real You

GETTING FROM A TO B

As many as I love, I rebuke and chasten.
Therefore be zealous and repent.

REVELATION 3:19

Each of us has experienced the touch of God on unyielded areas of our lives—areas where He wants to work a new depth of character, a new point of commitment, a new adjustment of our thoughts. The Lord is neither an unkind nor a hard taskmaster. But He knows there is no way for me to get from point A to point B in His purpose, apart from something happening in me. That "something" is described by one word in the Bible and one word alone.

It's the word *repent.*

A New Time and Place

GOD'S KINGDOM

*The eyes of the LORD run to and fro throughout
the whole earth, to show Himself strong on behalf of
those whose heart is loyal to Him.*

2 CHRONICLES 16:9

God is not democratic. His Kingdom is
not a democracy. He is never subject to our whim
or rule. The only real authority we ultimately have
with God is the right to completely rule Him out
of our lives. You can do that. But who in their
right minds wants to? That's the decision of those
who refuse Christ, who reject God's redemption
and rule through His appointed King.

But once I receive Jesus Christ as Savior, He
enters to become Lord. Once my choice is to "rule
Him *in*," He comes in to rule! He takes over at
Master-control and exercises God's Kingdom rule
to achieve our best blessing and highest destiny.

Taking Hold of Tomorrow

THINK AGAIN

The goodness of God leads you to repentance.

ROMANS 2:4

The Greek word for repent is *metanoeo,* which is a construct of the words *meta* meaning "after" and *noeo* meaning "to think." In other words, repentance is a decision on our part to "think again"—literally to have a change of mind that leads to a change of action. It is a decision to turn around and pursue another path.

Repentance is a deliberate act of the will as we decide to turn around and follow God's way instead of our own. Although repentance may involve emotion, it is primarily an act of volition.

Grounds for Living

Rich in Mercy

But God, who is rich in mercy, because of
His great love . . . made us alive together with Christ.

EPHESIANS 2:4–5

The mercy the Scriptures teach is completely compassionate, entirely benevolent, and is totally paid for. Best of all, it is an abounding trait of God Himself who is "rich in mercy." Even the facts of my failure-deserving-judgment are met by God's mercy. Astoundingly, His great kindness, manifest through this trait of His nature, makes it possible for righteousness and peace "to kiss" (Ps. 85:10).

If that weren't amazing enough, Scripture tells us that our Father's mercy endures forever!

With God, mercy isn't an uncertain option but a divine certainty. It is guaranteed compassion.

Moments with Majesty

THE RIGHT "STUFF"

[He] is able to do exceedingly
abundantly above all that we ask or think.

EPHESIANS 3:20

Have you ever found yourself shrinking from God's call—His prompting to believe, to step forward in faith, to answer a moment of commitment? Have you ever responded, "I'd like to, Lord, but You've got the wrong person. I don't have that kind of stuff in me!"

And that's just the point.

Jesus never calls us on the basis of the "stuff" we have in ourselves. It's always on the basis of what *He* can work in us by *His* power—by *His* Holy Spirit. He has the right "stuff," and He knows how to install it in each of us who will let Him have His way.

The Power and Blessing

GOD IN CREATION

The heavens declare the glory of God;
and the firmament shows His handiwork.

PSALM 19:1

One of the beauties of the Psalms is their affirmation that the physical realm gives eloquent testimony to the glory of God, that creation testifies to the grandeur of the Creator. We could take lessons!

The beauty of the sky bears witness to God's glory. The psalmist draws evidence of God's majestic glory from the beauty of a sunset and unending variations of cloud formations. These wonders call us to profound appreciation for the created order. We praise Him in humility before His glory and with a sense of responsibility—as stewards of this splendor.

The Heart of Praise

WE NEED EACH OTHER

*None of us lives
to himself, and no one dies to himself.*

ROMANS 14:7

We all need to learn to interrelate as members of Christ's Body. There are those around you experiencing the Holy Spirit's help toward their completeness, maturity, and wholeness in the same way He is helping you. For some things to get done in you, you have to recognize your brothers and sisters in Jesus. We cannot see our lives completed by ourselves. The Holy Spirit is our primary Helper, but He has willed to use us as instruments in each other's lives.

I need you to help complete what I'm to become. And you need me and others who touch your life to help complete what you are to become.

Rebuilding the Real You

GOD IS LOVE

*He who does not love
does not know God, for God is love.*

1 JOHN 4:8

God is love" is not an old saw, it is biblical affirmation. It does not depersonalize the Almighty by replacing Him with an idea or an emotion. To the contrary, it defines His nature.

"God is love" says that anything and everything that answers to the finest qualities of true love flows from Him. He is the source of all real love. He is also the judge of all that would call itself love and by its counterfeit seek to deceive minds and destroy hearts.

What is His call to us? "Beloved, if God so loved us, we also ought to love one another" (1 John 4:11).

Prayer Is Invading the Impossible

A Lamp, a Light

Your Word is a lamp to my feet and a light to my path.

PSALM 119:105

The direction that comes from God's Word is both immediately at hand as well as revealing what is distant. When the Bible says, "Your Word is a lamp and a light," the Hebrew words are the equivalent in today's technology to saying, "You'll have a flashlight in one hand and a giant spotlight in the other." Both aspects of my pathway come into view: *details* for today and *discernment* for tomorrow.

God's Word is essential to everything in our lives. Every issue of life is covered in this precious Book.

The Power and Blessing

WAITING ON THE LORD

*Those who wait on
the LORD, they shall inherit the earth.*

PSALM 37:9

Waiting upon the Lord" is an expression
that tends to sound contemplative and
introspective. Actually it's a summons to serve.
Servants "wait" on their masters, and "waiters"
serve their customers.

In praise, you and I are directed toward
faithful and powerful service. Praise announces
our entry into God's presence, purifies our
attitude, and insures our fulfillment while we
learn to wait in His presence.

Praise is right. Praise is lovely. Praise is
appropriate.

Prayer Is Invading the Impossible

"Hang in There!"

God is my strength and
power, and He makes my way perfect.

2 SAMUEL 22:33

God is looking for those who will move into partnership with Him in the struggle for mankind. He is searching for those who will grow up, who will lay hold of prayer responsibility, who will accept fundamental disciplines of the Jesus-life, who will give unselfishly, who will speak openly.

In short, God rejoices in people who "hang in there" because they know it will make a difference in their world.

He desires not only that we learn to *receive* His love but that we learn to *release* His love.

Moments with Majesty

WHO DO I SERVE?

As for me and my house, we will serve the LORD.

JOSHUA 24:15

What I am at home is what I *really* am:
The way I speak and act in private.
The material I read when I'm alone.

The music that fills my dwelling. The table-talk my family shares . . . or doesn't.

The moods I invite or tolerate. The entertainment I seek and foster. The media input I welcome.

The Savior I praise and worship . . .

That's the bottom line: Who am I serving, Him or me? As for me and everything in and about my house, *Jesus* will be central. We will worship Him; we will serve Him!

Taking Hold of Tomorrow

TRANSFORMED

We all, . . . are being transformed into the same image
from glory to glory, just as by the Spirit of the Lord.

2 CORINTHIANS 3:18

As God's servants, I see our twenty-first
century challenge not so much a call to greater
activity as a call to deeper transformation.
According to God's Word, "changed in His image"
people become the "shatter the darkness" people
(2 Cor. 3:18; 4:6). So "deeper transformation" isn't
an escape into philosophy, but an entrance into a
new availability—to Christ and to the world of
precious people He is seeking to save.

The Leading Edge

WAITING IN FAITH

*In the presence of Your saints
I will wait on Your name, for it is good.*

PSALM 52:9

How many times have you prayed, knowing full well that you have put the matter before God in faith, resting upon His Word . . . and nothing happens?

We live in an instant credit, get-everything-now society. We eat add-water-and-mix food or drive by fast-food outlets that poke our palates with immediate delicacies. All of this trains us to want what we want *now!*

Waiting is not in style, and patience has never been a forte of the flesh. But God has a great deal to say about waiting. His Word teaches that when nothing seems to be happening, something really is! Waiting is an opportunity to learn faith—the kind that grows, not just "gets."

Moments with Majesty

FORGIVE AND FORGET

If you bring your gift to the altar,
and there remember that your brother has something
against you, leave your gift . . . and
go your way. First be reconciled to your brother,
and then come and offer your gift.

MATTHEW 5:23

Relationship takes precedence over worship. That's shocking to our "spiritual" presuppositions, isn't it? But it's the Word of God from the lips of His Son. And it cannot be disregarded without paying the price of disobedience in prayer.

The penalty for violating this principle is more than merely not having my prayers answered. I find myself bound up in chains forged by my own unforgiving spirit. Grudge-bearing is a plague to the flesh. But my release of others is the pathway to being delivered from it.

When you're hurt by another forget it. *After* you forgive it!

Prayer Is Invading the Impossible

GOD'S FOREVER FAMILY

Grace be with all those who
love our Lord Jesus Christ in sincerity.

EPHESIANS 6:24

If we build homes that are aglow with God's love for one another, His light of truth shining from our windows and His grace pouring out toward our neighbors, the world will beat a path to our doors.

As individual parents and as vital congregations, the challenge of the new millennium calls us to build homes and families—havens of relational wholeness to which multitudes coming in from the cold of mangled relationships will be attracted, and thus find their way into God's forever family.

The Leading Edge

June

THE CROSS

HE BORE IS LIFE

AND HEALTH, . . .

HIS PEOPLE'S HOPE,

HIS PEOPLE'S

WEALTH.

GOD IS HERE

He has put a new song
in my mouth—praise to our God.

PSALM 40:3

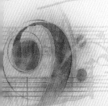 Praise in God's presence not only evicts the enemy's badgering, but erects a dwelling place for God's power. That's why He calls us to worship. He wants to meet with us and move among us. He wants to ignite the transformation of His people and initiate their interaction in His love.

Worship in God's mind is intended for encounter and action. He wants us to know He is neither inaccessible nor impersonal. He is here—and He wants to be invited to do something to us, in us, and among us.

Glory on Your House

HE VISITED US

Though He was a Son, yet He learned
obedience by the things which He suffered.

HEBREWS 5:8

In consenting to visit us, Christ placed Omniscience into the schoolroom of human experience. He who knows all, acknowledged His desire to learn, to discover human pain in a human body, to feel disappointment with human emotions, and to suffer human misunderstanding. He might have simply asserted His perception of these human sensations. His justice would have been no less righteous. He would not have been less loving, less holy, or less God had He never submitted to these things.

But He *did*.

The Visitor

GOD MAKES A WAY

Forever, O LORD, Your word is settled in heaven.

PSALM 119:89

The essence of prayer is this:

1. I accept the premise that God has decreed that certain matters are to be.

2. Whenever I encounter circumstance or situations in which His benevolent or righteous decrees are obviously not ruling, I pray.

3. My prayer calls forth what He has willed but cannot release on earth until someone here calls for it.

4. My prayer is prevailing prayer that continues relentlessly, all the while believing that the waiting is not worthless. God is working to make way for the release of the matter.

Prayer Is Invading the Impossible

CLOTHED IN CHRIST

Give unto the LORD the glory due to
His name; worship the LORD in the beauty of holiness.

PSALM 29:2

From one standpoint, we are exactly right when we feel we're too sinful to stand in the presence of God. But let us remember we worship "in Christ"—in the beauty of His holiness. Through Him we have been cleansed and are able to stand before the holy God.

If we dare to confess that we have been stained with sin, we can also believe with equal boldness that Christ's holiness will clothe us. In the beauty of His holiness—in robes of His righteousness—He enables us to stand high and lifted up before God.

The Heart of Praise

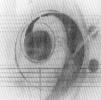

Move on to Tomorrow!

Forgetting those things which are behind . . .
I press toward the goal for the prize of the upward call
of God in Christ Jesus.

PHILIPPIANS 3:13–14

We can all remember instances from our past that prompt the thought of how different life might have been, "If . . ."

"If only this hadn't happened to me, I could have . . ."

"If only my folks had . . . "

"If only I'd had the chance . . . "

"If . . ."

In Christ, it's time to move on to tomorrow!

That's the message of the gospel. Our sins have been nailed to the Cross. Everything that would restrict our lives and limit our tomorrows has been cancelled. And what is true of our salvation and forgiveness is equally true of the practical details of our lives.

Taking Hold of Tomorrow

PERFECT BY GOD'S POWER

Having begun in the Spirit,
are you now being made perfect by the flesh?

GALATIANS 3:3

Once we have begun our life in Christ, each of us will sooner or later be confronted with a crucial question: Will I learn to live by the same power that birthed me into this new life? Since the power that brought the life of Christ to me was by the Holy Spirit, by what power will I grow in this life? The answer is rather obvious. By the same Spirit!

Paul wrote the Galatians, "Having begun in the [lifepower of the Spirit], are you now [by the energy of your own flesh] being made perfect?" We all need to answer that question. New birth isn't the end of God's program for us. His Spirit has started something powerful that He wants to continue throughout our lives.

Rebuilding the Real You

CHRIST DESTROYED DEATH

He who hears My word and
believes in Him who sent Me has everlasting life,
and . . . has passed from death into life.

JOHN 5:24

In becoming the ultimate casualty of sin—God dying for mankind—Jesus exhausted the dynamic of death in whatever form it may take: death of a soul, which sin works; death of hope, which despair brings; death of love, which strife produces; death of understanding, which bigotry accomplishes; death of comfort, with which pain torments us; death of body, which is mankind's final blow.

Every casualty of life's frustrations, dilemmas, weaknesses, temptations, sins, sicknesses, pains, sorrows, heartaches, and hopelessness is to be served notice: *Christ destroyed death for you!*

Prayer Is Invading the Impossible

PASSION FOR FULLNESS

*He who believes in Me, as the Scripture
has said, out of his heart will flow rivers of living water.*

JOHN 7:38

The passion for fullness is not a search
for some sensuous spiritual sensation. It's a quest
for God Himself—a return to the Fountain of our
being that the fullness of His purpose for us in
Christ might be realized.

Without restriction. Without inhibition.

There are no theological mysteries, administrative
techniques, ecclesiastical structures or marketing
techniques waiting to be discovered as keys to
tomorrow's triumphs. The passion for fullness is a
passion for God Himself.

A Passion for Fullness

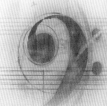

Love Without Measure

In this is love, not that we loved God,
but that He loved us and sent His Son to be the
propitiation for our sins.

1 JOHN 4:10

 Christ lives in me! This is eternal life. And what is the quality of that life?

We can speak of His love, without measure.

We can speak of His forgiveness, beyond comprehension.

We can speak of His healing touch, like no other.

We can speak of His shattering victory over death and Satan.

Eternal life begins the moment you acknowledge Jesus Christ as Savior and Lord. It's too big to wait until forever!

Glorious Morning!

STEWARDS OF BRIGHTNESS

Walk in the light as He is in the light.

1 JOHN 1:7

The talk, attitudes, and entertainment that characterize your home either pollute or illumine. It is important to cultivate a genuine mood of hope in your home. Hope is not a "cross-your-fingers" kind of dreamy-eyed sentiment. Hope is the solid conviction that God has a genuine, custom-made, blessed plan for you and your family, and that He is totally committed to seeing it fulfilled! When that idea dominates your heart it will light your life—and your house.

We are the stewards of this brightness.

Glory on Your House

SEEKING FOR SINNERS

The Son of Man has come
to seek and to save that which was lost.

LUKE 19:10

A person who walks into a coal mine while wearing a white linen suit is obviously more vulnerable and sensitive to the dusty environment than those who are always blackened by their toil there. So it was with Jesus when He plunged into the mineshaft of this world's sin. Though sinless in Himself, He "suffered" the presence of sin and temptation.

Yet, the even greater reality of Jesus' victory over sin's pressure and temptation is that while clothed in perfect purity and walking through the inky mine of all that provokes and produces human sinning, Christ continually embraced the sinful. He drew them to Himself and left each one imprinted with His holiness.

The Visitor

GO AHEAD AND DREAM!

*Great is our LORD, and mighty
in power; His understanding is infinite.*

PSALM 147:5

God calls us to give ourselves over to His will and with no guarantees—only His promises. And even then He doesn't promise a gold mine in every mountain He calls us to climb. But He does promise that if a mountain gets in the way of His purposed fulfillment for our lives, He can move it!

God never disallows dreams! In fact, He gives them. So He'll never tell us that we can't have dreams, desires, longings, or fulfillment. He only warns us against being controlled by the fear of not having them on our schedule or of seeking them on our own terms.

The Key to Everything

Search Me, O God

He who searches the hearts
knows what the mind of the Spirit is.

ROMANS 8:27

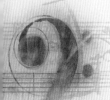 When we ask God to search the corridors of our lives, it isn't merely to have them swept clean but to rid us of anything that hinders His image being revealed in us. Becoming alert to the danger of deception is not simply a quest for being right, but a quest to allow His liberating truth-fullness to overflow our lives and make us free. Asking the Holy Spirit to guard our mouths and our hearts isn't an exercise born of fear, but a request based on our desire for the Wisdom of God—Jesus Christ—to be seen in our lives!

Our Daily Walk

WORSHIP IS SUBMISSION

*You shall worship the L*ORD
your God, and Him only you shall serve.

MATTHEW 4:10

Let's think through the basic meaning of one of the New Testament's primary words for worship: *proskeuneo,* which means "to prostrate oneself." It refers to the custom of bowing face down before God.

Of course the essence of falling on one's face is more than simply prostrating the body. It demonstrates submission of the will—a sign that we totally forfeit self will in favor of God's will. *Proskeuneo* worship implies absolute submission to the Lord.

The Heart of Praise

RUINED FOR SIN

Whoever abides in Him does not sin.

1 JOHN 3:6

 The original language of this verse actually says, "Whoever is born of God *does not keep on sinning!*" The words were not meant to say a new believer is never able to sin again, but that the life of God in you and me assures that we are on a path of growth that is relentlessly *reducing our capability to sin* as we did in the past!

In a very real sense, this passage of Scripture says, "Once I have been born again, I'm ruined for being the kind of sinner I was!" Hallelujah!

Rebuilding the Real You

GOD'S GLORY

Delight yourself also in the LORD,
and He shall give you the desires of your heart.

PSALM 37:4

We sell ourselves on the need to "help God work things out." We argue our need to make a change, add some excitement, or get something new going, because we're empty. Our tastes just aren't being satisfied where we are and with what we have. But the problem is deeper than an earthly "taste" can satisfy. Jesus calls you and me "children of the light" whom He longs to wean from dabbling in the darkness.

By welcoming His glory with our praise, the way is opened for God to plant the desires of His heart into ours. The fullness of God's life in us penetrates every hollow, hungry place, bringing fulfillment, joy, peace, and supreme satisfaction to our lives.

A New Time and Place

FAITH, HOPE, AND LOVE

Let us run with endurance
the race that is set before us, looking unto Jesus,
the author and finisher of our faith.

HEBREWS 12:1

 Are you experiencing one of life's bad days? Then let me invite you to come with me to the Cross, not to commiserate over agonies but to find companionship and direction. While the sum of human pain and problems is focused here— *all* suffering, *all* rejection, *all* painfulness, *all* exhaustion, *all* misunderstanding, *all* loneliness, *all* death—so is *all* wisdom and understanding, with *all* faith, hope, and love.

How to Live Through a Bad Day

A SONG OF PRAISE

*My tongue shall speak of Your
righteousness and of Your praise all the day long.*

PSALM 35:28

Let the spirit of praise rise to so great and tenderly loving a Father, Whose gentle grace reaches to us at every dimension of our need—spirit, soul, and body.

Let a song of praise rise to the Son, our Savior, Whose suffering incorporated a provision of healing for the whole person, as surely as His death has accomplished forgiveness and eternal life!

And let a welcome to the Holy Spirit be extended, to move among us as God's people in ways that continue, now and ever, to glorify the present ministry of Christ by manifesting His presence in our midst, and by distributing healing gifts in tribute to His glorious Name!

Grounds for Living

MERCY AND KINDNESS

He who honors [His Maker] has mercy on the needy.

PROVERBS 14:31

In His wisdom, God frequently chooses to meet our needs by showing His love toward us through the hands and hearts of others. We have all been at the mercy of love—a love that the "Father of mercies" (2 Cor. 1:3) has placed in our hearts.

We have all been the grateful recipients of an outflow of thoughtfulness and kindness. We have been blessed beyond our capacities to produce adequate words of thanksgiving to those who have prayed, cared, called, given, cooked, helped, encouraged us . . . and on and on.

It's wonderful to receive such mercy at the hands of God's children. It's more wonderful still to *be* the hand that reaches out in mercy.

Moments with Majesty

WE SAY, "YES"

I can do all things through Christ who strengthens me.

PHILIPPIANS 4:13

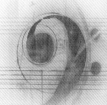 Real commitment is never a decision we make with fear's white knuckles or self-determination's grinding teeth, as though to say, "I'll try, God, but I don't know if I can make it!"

A holy and healthy commitment is made with our empty hands uplifted, saying, "You know best, Lord. I surrender to the possibilities You are calling me to. It's up to You!"

There's no end to what the Savior-Creator can remake with a surrendered soul wise enough to say, "Yes, Lord!"

The Power and Blessing

THE LORD'S SONG

How shall we sing the LORD's song in a foreign land?

PSALM 137:4

 How often life's moves and changes put us in a "strange land." But hear the psalmist, for he also understands: How difficult it is to sing the Lord's song in a strange land, when things become "foreign" to our plans.

Disappointing transitions, setbacks, and strange settings can spin our plans around and set our lives askew. Our challenge is to not allow circumstances to block our prayers or silence our praise.

You can be honest and admit that it's just easier to praise in some settings than in others. Then, go ahead and praise the Lord anyway!

The Heart of Praise

SONS AND DAUGHTERS OF GOD

Joined and knit together, . . . edifying . . . in love.

EPHESIANS 4:16

Years ago I was part of a reserve military training program. During my training, I was taught how a small team of soldiers—a squad—was to move forward in enemy territory. Each man had an assigned place in formation following the lead soldier. We were to proceed in such a way that we "covered" one another. Each soldier was responsible to maximize the safety and security of the others in his squad.

That is the essence of New Testament submission in relationships. It has nothing to do with reducing one another, but everything to do with protecting each other—being sensitive to one another, being sensible, and serving in our relationship to one another.

There are no *doormats*—only brothers and sisters in Christ, sons and daughters of the Father.

Rebuilding the Real You

TURMOIL OR TRIUMPH?

This is the love of God,
that we keep His commandments. And His
commandments are not burdensome.

1 JOHN 5:3

The whole purpose of God's commands is to keep us safe from the destructive power of sin, not to badger us with a land-locking set of rules that would take the wind out of full-sail living. God, who created us, knows what will best fulfill us.

Sin and Satan work disorder and confusion. God's ways are victory and life. He shows the way to surmount our own propensity for failure and heartbreak, and He enables us by His Spirit to overcome the slings of satanic fury bent on death and destruction.

Prayer Is Invading the Impossible

ALIGNED WITH GOD

Unite my heart to fear Your name.

PSALM 86:11

In English, *integrity* is a word related to a number of other familiar ones. It is built from the root word, *integer.* Now, as most of us learned in early math, an integer is a whole number, as in 1, 2, 3, 4—that is, whole numbers as opposed to fractions. They are whole or complete numbers, not parts of a whole.

In relating the word *integrity* to our lives, it describes an uncompromised character, an unjaded soul, an unsullied heart, and an undivided mind. It requires the maintenance of our hearts in entirety before the Lord. David said: "Unite my heart to fear Your name." Those words say, "God, draw the strands of my heart so firmly tight and in such reverence before Your throne, that I will be kept wholly and entirely aligned with You."

The Power and Blessing

Thanks in all Things

*In everything give thanks; for this
is the will of God in Christ Jesus for you.*

1 THESSALONIANS 5:18

The verse does not say, "Everything that occurs is God's will in Christ Jesus concerning you, so give thanks for everything." It says instead: "*In* everything give thanks—for that very spirit of praise is God's will in Christ Jesus for you." In other words, the Word of God does not command us to thank God for every heartrending pain, evil, tragedy, or trouble that crosses our paths. Instead it tells us to never let circumstances dampen our praise.

And the verse does not say "for" everything give thanks, but "in" everything. Whatever the situation, no matter how bleak, we are to praise God. Not for what He let happen, but that He is greater than the circumstance and that His love will guarantee our triumph over the test.

Prayer Is Invading the Impossible

PATHWAY OF PURPOSE

I delight to do Your will,
O my God, and Your law is within my heart.

PSALM 40:8

The pathway to heaven is paved with gold, purchased in full through the Cross and freely traversed by all who come to God through Jesus Christ. But the pathways to the world—paths He prods us toward as ministers of His life, His power, His love and His mercy—are rocky, thorn-strewn, and uphill all the way.

You eventually come to the place where you must make a decision: Will you simply take heaven as God's gift and receive His love solely as an individual . . . or will you take and receive all He offers and then—*and then*—give yourself back for His use and His purposes?

That's where discipline, faithfulness, service, and persistence come in.

Moments with Majesty

THE WAY OF THE CROSS

*He who does not take his cross
and follow after Me is not worthy of Me.*

MATTHEW 10:38

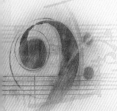 The Cross calls us to Jesus, who alone is the Way, the Truth, and the Life. Who alone holds the keys of eternal life and calls us to receive His forgiveness and power through our repentance for sin and faith in Him as God's Son, the only Savior. The Cross also calls us to *a life*. To the wisdom of God's ways in all our relationships and pursuits, and to the pattern of Jesus' model in the face of our deepest struggles and most difficult trials.

The charted course is clear. It is and always has been called "the way of the Cross." It is a way of surrender, of letting go.

How to Live Through a Bad Day

WAITING PATIENTLY

My soul, wait silently for
God alone, for my expectation is from Him.

PSALM 62:5

If God wasn't growing sons and daughters, things wouldn't take nearly as long. But since He is more interested in our *growing* than in our *getting*, waiting becomes an essential and useful means toward that end. He's not interested in add-water-and-mix saints, or in freezer-to-microwave-to-table kids. He takes the long view.

So what do you do while you're waiting?

Be *confident* that He takes no delight in compelling you to wait. He is, rather, patiently overseeing your life.

Rest. He wants you to trust Him.

Moments with Majesty

THE FATHER'S POWER

*Yours is the kingdom and
the power and the glory forever. Amen.*

MATTHEW 6:13

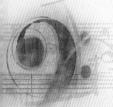 All prayer concludes by placing everything in God's hands.

Prayer must be filled with faith, uttered with boldness, offered in obedience, and overflowing with praise and confidence. But after all is said, it's still up to Him.

The answers may not come in the size packages you suppose, or be delivered at the moment you have in mind. But trust Him. All power and glory are His. And in speaking that with praise, you open the door to His invitation that you share it with Him, "in His way, at His time."

Prayer is Invading the Impossible

VICTORY

"Repent, for the kingdom of heaven is at hand."

MATTHEW 4:17

Victory is never far removed when repentance is given place. "Repent," Jesus says, "for the kingdom of heaven is at hand."

That Kingdom ushers in God's might, and hell doesn't stand a chance. You needn't fear the capability of God's power to bring deliverance and victory, no matter what the enemy may have accomplished to date, "because He who is in you is greater than he who is in the world!"

Bring to Him in full renunciation *anything* the Holy Spirit shows you is unworthy of God's child and the Cross will bring Christ's triumph wherever the power of His blood and name are declared. We are His *own,* and we are His *owned!*

Taking Hold of Tomorrow

July

FOLLOW CHRIST

TODAY UP THE

NARROW WAY

THAT LEADS TO

HIGHER GROUND.

HE LOVES YOU

I have loved you with an everlasting love;
therefore with lovingkindness I have drawn you.

JEREMIAH 31:3

Jesus came just to say, "I love you." It is perfectly appropriate simply to look into His face and let the full measure of His words touch your emotions. He does love you.

Deeply. And thoroughly.

And while you're praising Him for that, thank Him that He has also promised to abide with you forever.

Never leaving.

Never forsaking.

The Visitor

RELEASING GRACE

*Lead me in Your truth and
teach me, for You are the God of my salvation.*

PSALM 25:5

Our fears have taught us that to give anything is to be left with less, and to give everything is to be left with nothing. But this deep affliction—the tendency of the human soul to knot with spasms of clutching, cloying self-protectiveness—is a soul-sickness directly related to mankind's separation from God. Once the genuine rebirth of a human spirit occurs, the seeds of possible restoration of full freedom are sown.

Our new birth in Christ is only the starting place for growth in a life that can learn to live in the spirit of God's releasing grace, which causes us to give as we have received, forgive as we have been forgiven, and trustingly serve others with our God-given resources, gifts, and time.

The Key to Everything

JOY AND STRENGTH

The joy of the LORD is your strength.

NEHEMIAH 8:10

Whatever trial, tragedy, stress, or disappointment I may face, joy remains constant. It continues to rise from the well-spring of God's loving purpose for me—I am of Him, He is with me, and no matter what, I will be victorious.

Once that deep-seated confidence possesses you, and the conviction of certain triumph grips your soul, you come to understand the meaning of the eternal word: "the joy of the LORD is your strength."

Come. . . and Behold Him!

AN EXPRESSION OF GOD

If we live in the Spirit, let us also walk in the Spirit.

GALATIANS 5:25

Whether we may have recognized it or not, the Holy Spirit has at some time and in some way touched each of us.

The Holy Spirit is an expression of God,— He exists really, truly, actually, personally. He is not some abstract force or a distant cosmic influence. He is very personal, and as one expression of the Three-in-One God who created us, the Holy Spirit loves us—loves you!

He actively works to bring us into the knowledge of Christ. He processes redemptive grace toward us, and He longs to bring us to full maturity in life and to the realization of God's created purpose in each of us.

Rebuilding the Real You

Contracting with God

*Call to Me, and I will answer you, and show
you great and mighty things, which you do not know.*

JEREMIAH 33:3

Prayer cuts through the rag-tag affairs of
earth at their most decadent and lays hold of God's
sovereign order. He has established an order for all
things—an order determined before the world
began and decreed according to His eternal will.
Prayer calls forth from the Almighty the
reinstatement of His original decree in whatever
matters we bring before Him.

Since God has an intended purpose regarding
every specific matter, when we pray we are
contracting with Him for that purpose to be
fulfilled. This is in accordance with the authority
He has granted us through His Son Jesus Christ.

Prayer Is Invading the Impossible

LOVE FOR GOD'S FAMILY

Walk in love, as Christ also
has loved us and given Himself for us.

EPHESIANS 5:2

The passion for fullness is a passion fired by love—love for Christ, love for God's Word, and a loving will to learn greater love for all the members of the vast family of our Father. Jesus Himself established the criteria for our mutual acceptance: "He who is not against us is on our side" (Mark 9:40).

His is the Church because He is the Savior. Ours is to learn to love one another, because we have been "so loved."

A Passion for Fullness

LORD OVER LIFE

*We see Jesus, who was made a little lower
than the angels, . . . crowned with glory and honor.*

HEBREWS 2:9

Jesus is Lord over life's question marks—over uncertainties, over seasons of confusion and disorientation, over ignorance about where I'm headed. All these piled up clouds of anxiety are scattered to the winds by the sweet cry of joy that echoes through the centuries: He is alive! He is risen as He said!

Anyone who can descend into death, conquer hell and the devil, touch bases with earth and earthlings, and then spring heavenward into glorious rule at the right hand of All Power on high deserves my vote of confidence about handling my future—whatever it holds!

Glorious Morning!

KINGDOM PEOPLE

Freely you have received, freely give.

MATTHEW 10:8

Jesus shaped His disciples with spiritual readiness so they might love people in the middle of their need. He taught them to be confident when praying for the hurting, and to be sensitive when reaching out to those who showed a hunger for God's love. He was preparing Kingdom people— people who understand who they are and what they, as the Body of Christ, can become. Kingdom people move into each day as ordinary people, who can become naturally supernatural—that is, available to the Holy Spirit's direction and power.

Glory on Your House

SUSTAINED THROUGH SUFFERING

Since he himself has now been through suffering . . .
when we suffer . . . he is wonderfully able to help us.

HEBREWS 2:18, TLB

There is a force—a power—in Jesus' own suffering to break the ability of pain, injury, or sorrow to dominate us, even when these things seem to persist beyond prayer. Christ's suffering has the power to absorb the most hellish attack, the most tragic grief, the most traumatic pain, or whatever seems more than we can bear.

Jesus has broken the ability of suffering to reduce us to bitterness or disobedience. He wants to fill us with the same life that brought Him through suffering, that kept Him from growing weary in well doing.

The Visitor

OUR TREASURE

One's life does not consist in the
abundance of the things he possesses.

LUKE 12:15

If we ever put our resources, trust, confidence, identities or security in anything other than God, to that exact degree those things will become a substitute for Him. He won't allow that. It's the reason a covetous man is called an idolater (Eph. 5:5). The desperation and nervousness—the need to "have" that taunts us all—gradually will crowd God out completely. That's why possessiveness in any disguise must be identified, confronted, and surrendered to Him.

The Key to Everything

ONE DAY AT A TIME

Teach us to number our days and recognize
how few they are; help us to spend them as we should.

PSALM 90:12, TLB

The Bible is pointed about the value of each individual day and is equally direct in speaking of our responsibility to use these pieces of time wisely and profitably:

We are to consider each day a valuable gift, and look to God for wisdom in using that gift.

We are to treat each day separately, recognizing that "one day at a time" isn't just a clever slogan but a practical guideline to help us stay sensitive to today's duties and not worry about tomorrow.

Our Daily Walk

SING FOR JOY!

Sing out the honor
of His name; make His praise glorious.

PSALM 66:2

Both Judaism and Christianity are singing faiths. There are so many references to music and singing in the Psalms that they have been called Israel's hymnbook. The word *psalm* actually means "song," originally referring to the words sung to the accompaniment of a psaltery, an ancient stringed instrument. Psalm-singing was important from the very beginning of Christianity, especially to express the sheer exuberance and joy of a heart yielded to God.

You say you don't have a good voice? You don't know music? Remember. God likes your voice, so even if you never learn to carry a tune, use it. You carry around with you the most important instrument for singing—your heart!

The Heart of Praise

SOMETHING SPECIAL

*The LORD said to Joshua, "This day I will begin
to exalt you in the sight of all Israel, that they may know
that, as I was with Moses, so I will be with you."*

JOSHUA 3:7

There is something touching about this
statement, something that reveals the heart of
God's love.

God says, "Joshua, I'm going to make someone
important out of you!"

As you read those words, think with me of
those other words of Scripture: "God is no
respecter of persons." He does not value any of
His redeemed above another. That means, in
short, that if God said to Joshua He would make
something of special worth in him, so will He
with you and me!

Taking Hold of Tomorrow

CLOSE TO THE CROSS

You were bought at a price; therefore glorify
God in your body and in your spirit, which are God's.

1 CORINTHIANS 6:20

If you and I stay close to the Cross and to Jesus Christ who died there, who rose again, and now lives forever, we'll never lose sight of what was given at Calvary: *everything*.

And if we remember that,
we'll always remember to *for*give,
we'll never be afraid to *give*,
we'll have found the way to *live*.

We won't stop to count the cost of anything God asks us to do. It will never seem like a little or a lot because our lives will be lived in the light of the Cross—where everything takes on a different perspective.

The Key to Everything

PRAYING THE WORD

I will pray with the spirit,
and I will also pray with the understanding.

1 CORINTHIANS 14:15

The Holy Spirit wants to bring the Word of God to mind as we pray. Praying the Word leads us beyond mere humanistic ideas about God. Praying according to the promises of the Word reminds us that it is His nature to be good, loving, and merciful, so our prayer never bogs down in wonder about what God's will might be. He has revealed it.

His nature is to save, to heal, to rescue, to redeem, to provide, and to answer! The truths of God's Word say so, and by feeding upon them, we will soon find the truth and faith they bring filling our prayers.

Rebuilding the Real You

OUR REDEEMER RESTORES

He who has begun a good work in you will complete it.

PHILIPPIANS 1:6

All of us know what it means to lose. In one form or another, we've all tasted the bitterness of loss. We've all held the ashes of once-lovely dreams and felt them slip through our fingers.

But it is a constant in God's economy: What is lost may be reinstated, what is wasted may be recovered, and what is broken may be restored!

Above all expressions of His love, God, at heart, is a Redeemer—a Restorer!

A New Time and Place

Sing a New Song

Let the word of Christ dwell in you richly
in all wisdom, teaching and admonishing one another
in psalms and hymns and spiritual songs.

COLOSSIANS 3:16

In reading the writings of almost all great leaders, especially when discovering their own devotional practices, singing is recommended in one's private walk just as readily as it is an essential part of corporate worship. I always keep at least one hymnal at my place of devotion, and enjoy gaining inspiration from reading lyrics whether I sing them or not.

Alongside your hymnal, consider using your Bible as a source for singing in your private time with Jesus.

Be assured, though, Father God will receive any "new song" as a "sweet, sweet sound in His ear."

Pastors of Promise

THE SECRET OF FORGIVENESS

"Father, forgive them,
for they do not know what they do."

LUKE 23:34

Bad days are the results of things that happen, and things that happen are the results of what people do. People who misunderstand. People who intend to hurt us. People who forget or neglect to do something. People who betray or violate us.

Jesus teaches the secret of forgiveness: Forgiving those who hurt you is the key to not being permanently victimized by them. Whatever the initial impact of any offense you experience by others, your refusal to react, carry a grudge, or seek to retaliate in kind secures the high ground. But it must be as real as the Savior's forgiveness, not merely an exercise in self-control.

How to Live Through a Bad Day

THE GIFT OF GRACE

By grace you have been saved through faith,
and that not of yourselves; it is the gift of God, not
of works, lest anyone should boast.

EPHESIANS 2:8–9

Grace is the provision of God's work in place of ours. None of our works are effective in any way, but God's works are complete and all-powerful. The root meaning of this Greek word "grace"—*charis*—is "gift." A gift is something that is given without any condition. The only "condition" is that the giver loves the person he is giving the gift to and so decides to pay for it.

God loves you and has paid the entire bill for your salvation. That is grace. You can't do anything to earn it.

GRACE = **G**od's **R**iches **A**t **C**hrist's **E**xpense.

Grounds for Living

LET PEACE RULE

Let the peace of God rule in your hearts.

COLOSSIANS 3:15

The only thing that ever hinders peace is when we refuse to surrender our troubles to God. So, when dismay, frustration, or deep disappointments come, "Let the peace of God rule in your hearts." To surrender to God is never the same as surrendering to the situation—or to whatever works of hell may be afoot. It is an act of choice that overrules whatever of chance seems to be trying your soul, stretching your faith, or overthrowing your confidence.

Say, "Lord God almighty, I give this to You—completely!" Then with praise leave it there.

Moments with Majesty

PROMISE OF THE SPIRIT

Having received from the Father the
promise of the Holy Spirit, He [Jesus] poured out
this which you now see and hear.

ACTS 2:33

The blessing of being filled with the Holy Spirit is not for the sake of mere enjoyment. It is rejoicing, to be sure! But at the core of a life of growing discipleship with Jesus Christ, the Holy Spirit's work in our lives is what's most important.

It is the Spirit who keeps the Word alive.

It is the Spirit who infuses prayer and praise with passion.

It is the Spirit who teaches and instructs.

It is the Spirit who brings gifts and giftedness for power-ministry.

It is the Spirit who will bring love, graciousness, and a spirit of unity to our hearts.

The Power and Blessing

PRAISE IN PAIN

Return, O LORD! How long?
And have compassion on Your servants.

PSALM 90:13

The book of Psalms is a praise book for all seasons: when we rejoice in the Lord and exult over His providential care, and when our souls nearly burst with pain in times of darkness.

What can we do when life seems hard, defeating, unfulfilling, and aimless? Well, we can be honest in our prayers, as the psalmist was. We can cry to God, "Return, O LORD! How long? And have compassion on Your servants."

The writer isn't crying out in dark unbelief, but in the light of hope. In short, he is worshiping. The fact his heart isn't overflowing with blessing or abundance is no hindrance to his worship. It is all the more reason to seek solace and refuge in God.

The Heart of Praise

REBUILDING THE BROKEN

Neither death nor life, nor angels nor principalities
nor powers, nor things present nor things to come . . .
shall be able to separate us from the love of God.

ROMANS 8:38–39

Only God can so graciously yet wondrously
reverse circumstances caused by our own failures.

The Holy Spirit is able to recover, reclaim,
restore, renew, and rebuild whatever has been
broken. He will bring full restoration to your life,
your personality, your character, your mind—to
whatever part of you has been crushed, bruised,
broken, stained, tarnished, or ruined.

He can do that and He will. He will do that
even when some of the material is the broken
pieces of the life you bring.

Rebuilding the Real You

GRACE AND GOODNESS

*If by the one man's offense many died, much more
the grace of God and the gift by the grace of the one
Man, Jesus Christ, abounded to many.*

ROMANS 5:15

Let's get three things straight:

First, God is a good God.

Second, sin and Satan—flesh and Hell—have
fouled up God's intended processes for mankind.

Third, the redeemed—those who have
received God's gift of life in Jesus—are the main
channel of His dealing in grace and goodness on
this planet.

Prayer Is Invading the Impossible

"In Front of Jesus"

You are a chosen generation,
a royal priesthood, . . . the people of God.

1 PETER 2:9–10

Whenever Mamma thought I might be tempted to be less than truthful because of the pressure of a situation, she would say, "I'm going to ask you a difficult question, Jack. But before I do, I want to say, 'I'm asking it in front of Jesus.'"

And when Mamma would say, "In front of Jesus," I could just imagine Jesus seated on a throne immediately to my left as I stood face-to-face with Mamma, prepared to hear whatever question she asked.

There are no limits to what God can do in a life, what He can do through a life, and what He can grow around and within a life, when it's lived—*in front of Jesus.* That's the place where integrity of heart is always sustained.

The Power and Blessing

ASK WHAT YOU DESIRE

If you abide in Me,
and My words abide in you, you will ask what
you desire, and it shall be done for you.

JOHN 15:7

That verse is an uncanny declaration. Absolutely unbelievable.

Except, Christ said it—"ask what you desire."

And after all, He didn't sacrifice one iota of His own integrity by making that promise, because it is predicated on a significant premise: *abiding in Him.* That isn't some mystical position or some hard-to-arrive-at pattern of conduct. It isn't a religious accomplishment or a pious performance. It's just honest-to-God saying, "I want Your will."

His answer: "Pray, and I'll work it."

Prayer Is Invading the Impossible

PEACE OF MIND

You will keep him in perfect peace,
whose mind is stayed on You, because he trusts in You.

ISAIAH 26:3

To keep our hearts and minds under the protection and power of God's peace, we must fix our minds against a takeover by either anxiety or impurity (Phil. 4:6–8).

In short—whatever is hammering at your mind, your body, your family, your job, your life— God promises to keep you in perfect peace when you trust Him.

God will keep in perfect peace all those whose minds are stayed on Him. Set yourself in partnership with Him. The Prince of Peace is able to sustain peace in your life and mind, even in the face of the Enemy's evil efforts. The power is God's, but the vigilance is yours!

Moments with Majesty

PRAISE GOD

I thank You and praise You,
O God of my fathers.

DANIEL 2:23

Praising God in the midst of difficulty stakes out God's territory and power against Satan's.

I'm sure it wasn't easy for the three young Hebrews in the book of Daniel to praise God in the midst of the fiery furnace. They weren't praising the fire, but the presence of God with them in the fire. In times of difficulty, assert Jesus' overpowering presence with your praise and thanksgiving to Him.

The Heart of Praise

I HEAR A VOICE

My sheep hear My voice,
and I know them, and they follow Me.

JOHN 10:27

Jesus not only taught that sheep will know the shepherd's voice, He also declared, "My sheep hear My voice . . . and *they follow Me.*" He asserted that receiving His word—responding to it—is every bit as essential as recognizing it.

In describing the shepherd/sheep relationship as the basis for this order of hearing, He is saying: (1) If you don't listen, you won't know where He's going, and (2) if you don't respond, you won't be very close to where He is.

In other words, everything is at stake: His guidance and His glory. Without listening carefully, we can miss both.

Friends, I hear a voice. And I think you do, too.

Moments with Majesty

THE SPIRIT INTERCEDES

We do not know what we should pray for as we ought,
but the Spirit Himself makes intercession for us.

ROMANS 8:26

We don't know how to pray as we ought,"
the Scripture says, "so the Holy Spirit helps our
weakness by making intercessions." The Third
Person in the Godhead is active in (1) bringing to
mind people or circumstances we ought to pray
for, and (2) giving rise to prayer that exactly hits
the mark.

God Himself knows where hearts cry for His
intervention, and the Holy Spirit prompts us to
targeted prayer to release the working of God's
hand for them.

Prayer Is Invading the Impossible

CONSTANCY OF DEVOTION

We are members of His body.

EPHESIANS 5:30

Ephesians 5:20–33 not only points to the demanding nature of commitment needed by a husband and wife to make a marriage work, it also concludes with these sweeping words: "I speak concerning Christ and the church" (v. 32)!

The concept of true faith in Christ, and His faithful commitment to His own, is inextricably linked throughout God's Word to the figure of a faithful, growing marriage. Jesus communicated this idea in His parable of the returning bridegroom (see Matt. 25:1–3). His use of the figure fills the bridegroom/bride relationship with more than passion—the central issue is fidelity to a promise on the groom's part and constancy of devotion on the bride's. The message: Time can dampen fervor, but true love transcends emotion and remains committed.

The Leading Edge

August

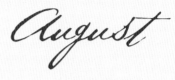

COME DWELL

IN ME, JESUS.

SAY WHAT

YOU WILL, JESUS.

DO ALL YOU

WANT TO DO.

CHRIST'S TRIUMPH

Do not be unbelieving, but believing.

JOHN 20:27

Into the panic-filled, upper-room, Jesus came to meet His disciples the evening following His resurrection. His approach shows the patience Jesus had with their fears, but it also shows how He aggressively presses the reality of His victory.

He invites them to examine His wounds, now so completely and miraculously healed. "Handle me," He says, urging them to fellowship by taking His hands, and to worship by coming to His feet. The reality of His triumph was verified. They touched the tangible evidence of a resurrected, victorious Savior!

Our Daily Walk

THE IMAGE OF GOD

*God . . . has in these last days spoken to us
by His Son, . . . the brightness of His glory and
the express image of His person.*

HEBREWS 1:1–3

Jesus is the express image of God. The Greek noun *karakter,* "image," was commonly used in the ancient world to describe the figure struck on a coin when minted. By its engraved authenticity and its stamped value, a coin declares its worth and its genuineness. And so it is with Jesus. When we look at Him we are seeing the full worthiness and the true magnificence of God. In Christ, all confusion as to what God is like is cleared up. Jesus is His "express image," the genuine article.

The Visitor

So Sincere

Incline your ear, and come to Me.
Hear, and your soul shall live.

ISAIAH 55:3

Sincerity, regardless how powerful it may be, cannot overcome the fundamental weakness sin brings to our nature. Charlie Brown says of his baseball team, "How can we lose when we're so sincere?" But lose they do, and likewise many sincere people lose sight of God's way of victory, drifting into deception without realizing they are off-target.

But if our hearts are open to God, and we acknowledge before Him our ability to be deceived, something wonderful happens. When we humbly and daily admit our need for His teaching, correction, and forgiveness, He responds to us and helps us past deception's blind spots.

Our Daily Walk

FREEDOM IS OURS

If the Son makes you free, you shall be free indeed.

JOHN 8:36

According to our Creator's intent, we ought to be free—free of sickness, torment, bondage, and confusion.

Yet because of another freedom He has invested in humankind—free will—that isn't always the case. Because of sin, men and women choose bondage over freedom . . . with tragic consequences.

But we can become as free as God intended when we receive His Son as our Savior. God has contracted for our redemption that we might enjoy every freedom and signed for it in His Son's blood. Intercessory prayer is the work of those who desire to see that contract fulfilled.

Prayer Is Invading the Impossible

GROWING IN GOD

The Spirit of truth . . .
dwells with you and will be in you.

JOHN 14:17

 The first thing to happen when a person comes to God and willingly receives the gift of life through Jesus, is that the Holy Spirit enters that person's life. Jesus described Him as a "Comforter"—literally, to define the Greek word *paracletos*—"One who remains beside you to help, to counsel, to teach and to strengthen you."

His entry, though, is just the beginning. As surely as we open to His incoming, we are also invited to open to His overflowing—continually. His mission is to help us onward as growing sons and daughters of the Most High God.

Rebuilding the Real You

A DAILY PRACTICE

Is anyone among you suffering? Let him pray.
Is anyone cheerful? Let him sing psalms.

JAMES 5:13

In nearly every page of God's Word we see that one thing begets the power to wreak havoc in the world of those bound by sin:

Prayer in response to an appointment by the Lord.

Prayer as a corporate response in a crisis.

Prayer as a daily practice.

Praise as a point of praiseful rejoicing.

Prayer as an expression of worship.

Prayer as a simple utterance spoken by but one in a time of need.

Prayer. Prayer. Prayer.

Prayer Is Invading the Impossible

LIGHT OF THE WORLD

Let us walk in the light of the LORD.

ISAIAH 2:5

White "light" is not the absence of color but actually the convergence of all colors. And we've all seen what happens when a beam of light is split. Passing through a prism—whether in the form of raindrops, an angular piece of glass, a crystal jewel or morning dew on a blade of grass— light separates into its component colors, and there before us, in the splendor of the spectrum, is the manifold brilliance of the rainbow.

So it is with our Lord Jesus Christ—the Light of the world. Sent by the Father into our world in His pristine, white-light perfection, He is the composite of the spectrum of God's fullness.

A Passion for Fullness

RECEIVE YOUR REDEEMER

Beauty for ashes, and the oil of joy for mourning.

ISAIAH 61:3

Whatever your loss, pain, or failure, Jesus Christ is fully capable of bringing about change unto full restoration. Just as His resurrection power brings new life, His redemption power brings new hope. He is able, for He's more than a Savior! He's your Redeemer who promises to give "beauty for ashes, and the oil of joy for mourning."

Just as you gave Him your heart and received Him as Savior, give Him your life's broken pieces. Receive Him as Redeemer.

Glorious Morning!

RESTORED AND RECONCILED

We rejoice in God through our Lord Jesus Christ,
through whom we have now received the
reconciliation.

ROMANS 5:11

Jesus came as both Savior and King. His mission was twofold. First, as the "second Adam" He came to rescue mankind and through His death to restore our relationship with the living God. Second, as resurrected Lord He has risen to begin the reinstatement of mankind to His intended estate as a "ruler-in-life" under God (Rom. 5:12).

Jesus summoned people to repentance and forgiveness, while He also showed them evidence of the transforming power of the Kingdom. He did that by restoring fallen humans through love, grace, and forgiveness, and by casting out the powers of darkness through mighty miracles and healings.

Glory on Your House

SHARE GRACE

*That we may be able to comfort those
who are in any trouble, with the comfort with which
we ourselves are comforted by God.*

2 CORINTHIANS 1:4

Jesus is looking for people who will minister His life, His truth, and His love to others in the same spirit that He ministers to us. He is always patient with those who are suffering. He offers full healing and complete deliverance.

He calls us to be that way with one another. He points the way for us to share with others in their suffering in the same way He has shared with us—in understanding and grace.

The Visitor

FAITHFUL STEWARDS

All things come from You,
and of Your own we have given You.

1 CHRONICLES 29:14

Banks fail. Investments fall apart. The continuous climb of inflation reduces the power of money saved today against tomorrow. These facts don't argue against saving or investment, but they do remind us it's impossible to be truly secure on earth's terms.

But once our trust is fixed completely in God, our living, loving Father will show us precisely how to manage our personal responsibilities. In His Word and by His Spirit, He teaches us how to be wise, disciplined, and faithful as His stewards, looking toward our future with faith, not fear.

The Key to Everything

Wisdom Each Day

He will teach us His ways,
and we shall walk in His paths.

 "Today" is always bright with promise and weighed down with duty. It's as easy to spend it profitably as it is to waste it. The wise thing to do is to bring each day to the Lord and ask Him about its intended purpose and best use.

Learn to systematically and personally present the details of each day to Him in prayer. Acknowledge Him as your Lord and Master at the beginning of every day. His wisdom and provision are readily available when you ask for them.

Our Daily Walk

GOD'S WILL BE DONE

I bow my knees to the Father
of our Lord Jesus Christ, from whom the whole
family in heaven and earth is named.

EPHESIANS 3:14

The incarnation shows that God has willed to work all redemptive operations through His children. And the establishment of the Church is the evidence that both the Father and the Son want that process to flow now through its agency. God works redemption through the Church (Eph. 3:10), which is people who call upon His rule to invade the mischievous and the merciless works of satanic power.

Jesus says, when you pray, and after you have come before the Father with worship, begin to call for His will to be worked on earth. That's the only way it's going to happen here—when those who want His will to be done declare that it be.

Prayer Is Invading the Impossible

SONGS IN THE NIGHT

*The LORD will command His lovingkindness in the
daytime, and in the night His song shall be with me—
a prayer to the God of my life.*

PSALM 42:8

Song comes from a different reservoir in
our brains than speech. Psychologists tell us that
music comes from the right side of the brain.

It is one of God's great blessings that the right
hemisphere of the brain is also the seat of many of
our emotions, not all of which stay upbeat all the
time. How gracious for God to locate a soothing
balm for our sorrow as well as a release for our joy
right alongside one another.

It is a gift from the One who flows light into
darkness and gives songs in the night.

The Heart of Praise

STAYING ON TRACK

Teach me Your way, O LORD; I will walk in Your truth.

PSALM 86:11

Constancy to God's Word brings success in life—the success born of obedience. Faith is not so much the power to acquire or to bring something *into* my life, as it is the power to obey God's plan *for* my life. To walk by faith is to stay on God's ordered paths, which naturally lead to the things He has planned—things that will fulfill us and make us fruitful servants.

Faith isn't an effort to acquire things by bursts of spiritual energy. It is simply staying on track in the pathway God's Word has ordained. Faith isn't a ritual of speech as much as a response in obedience. God's promises are already there in the path of His will for your life. Faith simply walks forward, moving in His way.

Taking Hold of Tomorrow

THE WHOLE IDEA

Thanks be to God who always leads us
in triumph in Christ, and through us diffuses the
fragrance of His knowledge in every place.

2 CORINTHIANS 2:14

The Holy Spirit desires to bring each of us to completion in Christ. This practical pursuit—our partnering with Him as He comes to help—is geared to make us whole or holy. That's what holiness is really about—wholeness.

The Holy Spirit comes:

to bring the *whole* life of Jesus Christ,

into the *whole* of our personalities,

so the *whole* love of God

can be relayed to the *whole* world!

The *whole* idea is holiness.

Rebuilding the Real You

PROMISED POSSIBILITIES

Through love serve one another.

GALATIANS 5:13

To think of the biblical term *harvest* is to think of people helping people, touching people, loving people, serving people, and winning people into the love of God. On the other hand, to misplace or lose our perspective on the harvest—on serving people with life—is the surest way to short-circuit the promised possibilities of our own lives.

I've found a common element in every individual who grows bitter, misses fulfillment, becomes sour, complains about God, falls into self-pity, or wonders "why nothing ever happens to me." That common denominator is a lost sense of ministry . . . of serving, loving, helping, and reaching others in the Savior's name.

A New Time and Place

READ THE WORD

Open my eyes, that I may
see wondrous things from Your law.

PSALM 119:18

We cannot live the Word, apply the Word, or pray the Word if we do not first read the Word. And our capacity to apply the Word effectively will be equal to our willingness to wait long enough in the Word for the Holy Spirit to enlighten our minds in its promises.

So take God's Word today and make it a primary part of your praying. You might pray what John Calvin often prayed before reading God's Word:

Heavenly Father, in whom is the
fullness of light and wisdom, enlighten my
mind by Your Holy Spirit, and give me
grace to receive Your Word with reverence
and humility. Living and Praying in Jesus' Name

FORGIVING FREELY

If you forgive men their trespasses,
your heavenly Father will also forgive you.

MATTHEW 6:14

 Forgiving others springs out of my gratitude to God for His forgiving me. True forgiveness is born of my remembrance that I've been forgiven so great a debt through God's love, there is no justification for my being less than fully forgiving of others. Because I have "freely received" God calls me to "freely give." To forgive those seeking to injure you or me is to remove ourselves from their counsel and to be unfettered by anger, pain, or disappointment.

How to Live Through a Bad Day

REFLECTING GOD'S GLORY

We all, with unveiled face, beholding as in a mirror the glory of the Lord, are being transformed into the same image from glory to glory, just as by the Spirit of the Lord.

2 CORINTHIANS 3:18

The Holy Spirit comes to restore the image and likeness of the Lord in us. We are changed into Christ's likeness as the Spirit works in us. God desires that we not only come to the Cross and have our sins forgiven, but that we also come and look in the "mirror" of His Son revealed in His Word, so we begin to be transformed.

The word *mirror* conveys the idea of "reflection" as well as "looking into." The more we look at the "mirror" of the Word that reflects God's glory, the more we will be changed into His image and likeness.

Grounds for Living

His Appointment

The mountains shall depart and the hills
be removed, but My kindness shall not depart from you.

ISAIAH 54:10

Neither a simple glitch in my plans nor an absolute barricade means life is ended. Our lives are in God's hands—no matter what.

Stand in faith! We cannot see the way God is going to work from where we are right now, but be sure, He will: "For the mountains shall depart and the hills be removed, but My kindness shall not depart from you."

Disappointment is changed by altering only one letter—the first one—to "H." Turn *dis*appointment into *His* appointment. Then, stand still and watch Him keep His appointment with your destiny.

Moments with Majesty

GOD WITH US

That I may dwell among them.

EXODUS 25:8

Salvation is God's grand design for recovering His original plan: *God tabernacling with man!* Whether it was God-with-man in the Garden or God-visits-man in the tabernacle or temple, the intent with the Father has always been, "That I may dwell among them."

So it is that in Immanuel (God with us), Jesus our Lord came to dwell among us, that He might multiply His life, person, and grace in each of us by the power of His salvation through the blessing of His incarnation.

According to the Word of God, the plan is working!

The Power and Blessing

PRAISE IS BEAUTIFUL

It is good to sing praises to our God;
for it is pleasant, and praise is beautiful.

PSALM 147:1

Beauty may not be your first thought when you get up in the morning and stare into the mirror. Stress, tragedy, or deep sorrow may have etched creases of weariness or suffering on your face. But make this experiment; prove God's Word. Take that countenance, as it is, into the presence of the Lord day after day, in frequent, steadfast praise and worship. The prophet Isaiah says plainly what you will receive in return. He says the Messiah is sent specifically to console those who mourn with "beauty for ashes, the oil of joy for mourning" (Isa. 61:3). That's an oil that surpasses the anti-aging effects of the best cosmetics!

The Heart of Praise

PROMISES WAITING

*Hope does not disappoint, because the
love of God has been poured out in our hearts.*

ROMANS 5:5

Hope is in the breath of the Holy Spirit.
Hope is yours and mine to keep—and to know
we'll never be embarrassed by God for having
hoped in His grace!

To cling to hope is to cling to the Lord. Hope
is born of the certainty the Holy Spirit wants to
instill in us—to know God already has the situation
in hand. The future is settled in His mind. And to
hope is to embrace the confidence that everything
God has promised to *be* already exists. All that
remains for us to do is to keep walking forward with
Him until we come to the place where each fulfilled
promise is already waiting.

Rebuilding the Real You

Our Blessed God

*The law is good . . . according
to the glorious gospel of the blessed God.*

1 TIMOTHY 1:8, 11

 The word *blessed (makarios)* in this verse also means "happy." The good news of the gospel spread by the early Church was that there was a loving and good God unlike the pagan deities, who plagued man with trickery and whose "happiest" moments of sexual indulgence or drunken revelry were always exchanged for disappointment and despair.

Our "blessed God" is that One who is bent on our fulfillment and happiness.

Prayer Is Invading the Impossible

TRUE SUBMISSION

*All of you be submissive to
one another, and be clothed with humility.*

1 PETER 5:5

True submission can never be forced, because, foremost, submission is always an inner attitude—a heart issue. It can never be *required*: it can only be *volunteered*—given as a willing gift. Only I can choose whether or not I will submit.

Under Christ, we must learn the spirit of submission as it relates to others—others we serve with, others we serve under, others we don't want to serve at all. But willingness, humility, and servant-hood must be kept in view.

I may say I'll "submit," but if my heart rankles and internally resents or resists, I'm not accepting or participating in the spirit of submission. And not only will I fail to experience God's power, I'll miss God's blessing.

The Power and Blessing

SACRIFICE FOR SIN

*If anybody does sin, we have one who speaks
to the Father in our defense—Jesus Christ, the
Righteous One. He is the atoning sacrifice for our sins.*

1 JOHN 2:1–2, NIV

Although the Heavenly Father does not hold a casual attitude toward sin, He is not shocked by it either. He has made provision for it, not as an invitation to sin, but to receive His freedom from its tragic consequences.

We make a serious mistake if we think God's mercy is the result of some "smile-and-forget-it" bend in His nature.

God's forgiveness is available and adequate because it cost an inestimable price: the blood of His Son.

Prayer Is Invading the Impossible

HE'S ALWAYS THERE

In the world you will have tribulation;
but be of good cheer, I have overcome the world.

JOHN 16:33

I am becoming more and more impressed with the summons to simplicity that Jesus issues: "Follow Me . . . trust Me . . . learn of Me. . . ." He makes no grand promises of a rose-strewn pathway. He doesn't roll out a blueprint of predictable details forecasting our tomorrows. Nor does He guarantee that we will ever arrive at some comfortable state of perfected accomplishment. Rather, He says, "In the world you will have tribulation."

But He's always there. That's what makes any season of trial, any call to faith, any burden of responsibility a glory time. Jesus is there. Not a doctrine about Him. Not an idea of what He's like. Not a memory of some past experience.

No. Just Him.

Moments with Majesty

REASON TO REJOICE

Let all those rejoice who put their trust in You;
let them ever shout for joy, because You defend them.

PSALM 5:11

 Eternal love shines from a cross and an empty tomb. Once Jesus died in our place and rose again to God's right hand, there is no power of defeat or distress that cannot be reversed! Listen . . . if death itself can be swallowed up in life, then every dead-end street in our sin-darkened world can be broken through! God's pathway of promise becomes a living highway of Kingdom victory.

The Kingdom comes with the King—and all of us who have welcomed Him into our hearts have reason to rejoice.

A New Time and Place

TRUE SPIRITUALITY

He who abides in Me, and I in him, bears
much fruit; for without Me you can do nothing.

JOHN 15:5

Jesus says, "He who abides in Me . . ." will
see things happen. Association—a constant link—
with Him will produce dissociation—a
consuming break—with everything in us that
isn't of Him. And when He makes us what God the
Father designed us to be, we are relieved of the task
of trying to appear to be something we *thought* we
should be.

True spirituality just happens. Like fruit on a
tree. Like flowers on a plant. I've never seen a
grape with a hernia . . . or a halo, for that matter.
They neither grunt nor glow . . . they just grow.

That's what "being spiritual" is all about.

Moments with Majesty

AN INTERCEDING CHURCH

If you ask anything in My name, I will do it.

JOHN 14:14

It is staggering to realize that the process by which God's will is done on earth depends on an interceding Church.

God is always consistent with His own regulations. By sheer right of His sovereignty He could do anything, anywhere, at anytime, by any means. But He doesn't. He confines Himself to the redemptive process worked through the Cross of His Son and released by the ministry of the Holy Spirit through the praying Church. He will do nothing outside those channels. That is not to say there is nothing else He could do; it is simply to say there is no other way that He will.

Prayer Is Invading the Impossible

September

JESUS,

LIFE IS

WHAT YOU

BROUGHT US;

TRUTH

YOU TAUGHT US.

CLOSE TO GOD

When you draw close to God, God will draw close to you.

JAMES 4:8, TLB

 Although God is willing to draw close to us, there is a scriptural condition to His doing so. We must draw close to Him. He is ready, even warmly anxious, to respond to us—but He awaits invitation. It is not a matter of God requiring protocol, as though He were a cosmic prima donna or a celebrity. He doesn't have the temperament for such contrived games. But He does know the human heart. And He knows that only those who take the first step of faith and surrender to Him can receive all He wants to give.

Our Daily Walk

LIFE, LIGHT, AND LOVE

*With great power the apostles gave witness
to the resurrection of the Lord Jesus. And great
grace was upon them all.*

ACTS 4:33

The book of Acts shows us believers who invaded the impossible. They prayed, then commanded cripples to walk. They prayed, and then marched into a pagan world with truth.

Their prayers brought life into the strongholds of death.

Their prayers brought light that drove darkness away.

Their prayers brought love to a world broken in sin.

The great grace that was upon them now rests upon us . . . and our prayers, too, will bring life, light, and love into our world.

Prayer Is Invading the Impossible

ABOUNDING PROVISION

No good thing will He
withhold from those who walk uprightly.

PSALM 84:11

Boaz, a marvelous Old Testament picture of our Lord Jesus Christ, reveals his love for Ruth, an equally beautiful picture of the Church, that is, of you and me. As they are about to become engaged, Boaz expresses his commitment to Ruth by asking her to spread out her shawl (see Ruth 3:15–18). Into its folds he pours out six ephahs of grain—a total of about seventy pounds of barley!

Now catch the picture. Can you see our Lord Jesus saying the same thing to us, His bride? "I don't want you to go through life empty-handed. I want you to know My abounding provision for all matters of your life." Jesus is saying, "I will fill the biggest pocket you've got! I'll fill it with love and everything else you need as well." That's His promise!

The Key to Everything

THOUGHT-FILLED WORSHIP

*Whatever things are true . . . noble . . . just
. . . pure. . . lovely . . . meditate on these things.*

PHILIPPIANS 4:8

Thinking carefully about the attributes of God as we praise Him is a way of offering Him our minds. When we hear the psalmist say that God is "above all gods," let's try to wrap our minds around His *omnipotence*—the fact that He is all-powerful.

Let's contemplate His *omnipresence*. He is everywhere present. He's inescapably, marvelously near, all at once. And think on our God, the one God who alone is *omniscient*—knowing all there is to know, now and forever. What an absolutely mind-boggling thought!

Thought-filled worship will not lift us with pride. It will drive us to our knees!

The Heart of Praise

A WORK OF WHOLENESS

*May the God of peace Himself sanctify you completely;
and may your whole spirit, soul, and body be preserved
blameless at the coming of our Lord Jesus Christ.*

1 THESSALONIANS 5:23

Your soul is made up of:

a. Your intellect—how you think.

b. Your emotions—how you feel.

c. Your will—the choices you make.

All three are addressed in Paul's prayer: "May your whole spirit, soul and body be preserved blameless at the coming of our Lord Jesus Christ." The Holy Spirit is still answering that prayer today. So boldly join your prayer to that one: "Oh, God, according to Your promise, I welcome your Holy Spirit to teach, to strengthen, to console, and to restore me. Work Your wholeness in my personality and make me like Jesus." Amen!

Rebuilding the Real You

UNITY OF THE BODY

Holy Father, keep through Your name those whom
You have given Me, that they may be one as We are.

JOHN 17:11

There is no question Jesus' prayer for unity is for greater reasons than mere togetherness. He knew the flow of His power would only be diminished by any fragmentation of His Body. His focus on His Body's unity was not political but practical—that all the world with all its need might have all He has to give through all His people!

That's why we are wise to pursue so complete a passion for Him that it melts any obstacles between us and any who love Him. A passion for God's fullness brings a loving willingness to learn greater love for all the members of His vast family.

A Passion for Fullness

A Friend for the Journey

Behold, I stand at the door and knock. If anyone hears My voice and opens the door, I will come in to him and dine with him, and he with Me.

REVELATION 3:20

 Wherever you may be, in whatever situation you may find yourself today, Jesus will step right in as you open the door to Him. He will enter with salvation. He will enter with healing. He will enter with strength, and counsel, and matchless wisdom. Whether you realize it or not, whether you recognize Him or not, He has been traveling with you on your long and winding journey.

It's time to invite Him in.

Glorious Morning!

THE KING'S BUSINESS

"Do business till I come."

LUKE 19:13

The advent of the Holy Spirit at Pentecost launched the Church. He anointed every member with the King's anointing, ensuring that His Kingdom would travel in them, giving them ability to deal with situations they would encounter in daily living.

The Church is comprised of people who have been (1) born of the same Spirit who begot Jesus; and (2) empowered by the same Spirit who empowered Him. Born of and baptized with the Spirit, the Church is assigned to do business— to operate with all God's gracious power until the King returns!

Glory on Your House

The Highest Potential

*Jesus Christ, . . . has abolished death and
brought life and immortality to light through the gospel.*

2 TIMOTHY 1:10

 Scripture says that Jesus brought life and immortality at His appearing.

Immortality has to do with our forever future.

Life is what is happening here and now.

Jesus offers us a quality of life never before possible for the children of Adam and Eve. It is life of the highest potential, possibility, and expectancy. It hints at a nobility and beauty beyond the reach of normal human experience.

Glorious Morning!

WE ARE HIS TEMPLES

*Do you not know that
your body is the temple of the Holy Spirit?*

1 CORINTHIANS 6:19

Jesus came in a human body to fulfill a precise aspect of the Father's will. The wounds sustained in His body are to break the shame of past sins performed by our bodies, blotting out that which often causes us to feel disqualified from being used by God. His physical wounds establish the Father's full possession and dominion in our bodies, as certainly as His forgiveness does in our souls.

Your body has been sanctified, made worthy by God Himself to be a residence of His Holy Spirit, a temple for His indwelling. Your physical frame, whatever its past abuse or present weakness, is being raised by the Holy Spirit as a shrine unto the God of the heavens!

The Visitor

A Future Without Fear

Do not worry about tomorrow.

MATTHEW 6:34

 Jesus wasn't saying we shouldn't plan or make any calculations about the future. He was telling us not to let our minds be hassled or pressed by how we're going to make it. In other words, we aren't to plan for our future in fear, doubt, or with selfish concern. We're to seek the Lord for specific direction and guidance, realizing that He will preserve both our future and our present. Then we're ready to carry out His purposes in confidence and faith.

The Key to Everything

LIGHT OF GOD'S LOVE

Commit everything you do to the Lord.
Trust him to help you do it and
he will. Your innocence will be clear to everyone.
He will vindicate you with the blazing light of justice
shining down as from the noonday sun.

PSALM 37:5–6, TLB

Note the words "with the blazing light" and "from the noonday sun." They signal a promise. The simple action of committing your day to God is a guarantee of blessing. The Lord's increased brightness will fill your days until every shadow is gone! Just as irresistibly as the sun rises and masters the darkness, our Lord will bring the effects of His loving purpose into our daily lives.

Our Daily Walk

GOD'S CHOIR

I will declare Your name to My brethren;
in the midst of the congregation I will praise You.

PSALM 22:22

God "inhabits the praises of Israel" (Ps. 22:3)—the gatherings of His people. The drama of worship is too grand a production to be produced by believers in lonely isolation from one another. So David worships on the hillsides, alone, but also says, "I will declare Your name to My brethren; *in the midst of the congregation* I will praise You."

Just as the church choir is composed of multiple voices, so every one of the diverse gifts in the congregation is essential for worship. You may not be gifted as a soprano, alto, tenor or bass, but you are gifted—and your gift is needed in God's choir!

The Heart of Praise

His Best—Our Blessing

He will love you and bless you and multiply you.

DEUTERONOMY 7:13

In the strictest of terms, Jesus as "Lord" is our *Owner*—even as serfs under ancient landlords were at the mercy of the owner of the fiefdom. They could be rewarded if he were benevolent, exploited if he were selfish.

Our submission to Jesus' lordship holds no uncertainty in that regard. As the One who holds the power over those submitted to Him, He delights to bless and protect, to prosper and enrich all who acknowledge His lordship.

Jesus our Lord wants to bless you. He wants to rule in your life to protect you from foolishness and evil, and to fulfill your highest possibilities. That's Christ's lordly style, and that's why He wants your submission. True submission makes way for His best to become our blessing!

Taking Hold of Tomorrow

COMPLETE IN HIM

As He who called you is holy,
you also be holy in all your conduct.

1 PETER 1:15

Holiness involves the idea of *completion* in all aspects of your being:

Your spirit can be revived to life in God (made holy).

Your soul (mind and emotions) can be restored (made whole).

Your physical body, habit, and conditions can become disciplined and recovered to well-being (kept healthy).

Holiness, or full recovery of spirit, soul, and body is for *now.* It is something God will do in us, bringing peace, completeness, and wholeness to our lives. In short, God's program of sanctification means He's ready to do everything He can to put us fully together *today!*

Rebuilding the Real You

THE WILL OF GOD

*It is God who works in you both
to will and to do for His good pleasure.*

PHILIPPIANS 2:13

So many people sit in my office and moan, "Oh, if only I could find the will of God for my life!"

Yet the will of God is found in your own heart.

You can get good counsel, read helpful books, and diagram your life on the kitchen table, but ultimately, the answer is in your heart. And when your heart is totally committed to follow Christ and walk in His ways, you can't miss the will of God. He'll get you there one way or another. Yes, the route may be roundabout. It may include a climb over some jagged mountains and dip down through some dry, rocky valleys. But God, who knows both the beginning and end of your days will get you there!

A New Time and Place

CLOTHED WITH MAJESTY

The LORD reigns, He is clothed with majesty.

PSALM 93:1

 To say our Lord is "clothed with majesty" is to say that all creation is window dressing for His excellence. It all points to Him. And just as a king's palace with all its royal décor reflects something of that king's personality, so creation reflects the magnificence of our Lord's nature and character.

But more amazing is the fact that God, who is clothed with majesty, chose to become the personification of majesty when He came to earth in the form of His Son, Jesus Christ. Jesus is the ultimate essence of God's glory and the personification of His immeasurable majesty.

Living and Praying in Jesus' Name

OUR TEACHER

I will instruct you and
teach you in the way you should go.

PSALM 32:8

The disciple's cry is, "Lord, teach me to pray."

The disciple's Lord says, "I will instruct you and teach you."

The Teacher never ends this lesson—"school" opens each morning for a lifetime. The student may be faithful or irregular in attendance, but the Teacher is always there—and always ready to spend all the time we need to "walk with Him and talk with Him." In those moments, His promise of a lifetime of purpose, fruitfulness, fulfillment, and victory is renewed in our souls.

Pastors of Promise

FREEING FORGIVENESS

If you do not forgive men their trespasses,
neither will your Father forgive your trespasses.

MATTHEW 6:15

People turn on people. Crass unkindness, vicious plottings, horrible and intentional antagonisms happen, and a bad day hardly describes the extended season of a struggle many of us face at times. But there is a lesson at Calvary.

Forgive everyone—anyone—whom you think has failed you, hurt you, offended you. If you think others have done anything to ruin your life, ruin your day, ruin your opportunities, ruin your dreams, or block your goals, forgive them. Forgiving others is the key to living in the liberty of the freeing forgiveness Jesus has given to us.

How to Live Through a Bad Day

POWER AND TENDERNESS

In Him we have redemption through His blood, the
forgiveness of sins, according to the riches of His grace.

EPHESIANS 1:7

The word *forgiveness* is unquestionably one
of the loveliest words in the Bible. It represents
both the power and the tenderness of God. It is as
strong as steel and as soft as velvet.

There is a glory about the truth of forgiveness
that touches the deepest places of our hearts. The
precious blood of Christ not only paid the price
for our forgiveness but broke the power of sin in
our lives, and broke the power of the enemy to
bring condemnation upon our heads.

Grounds for Living

ANCHOR OF ASSURANCE

*This hope we have as an anchor
of the soul, both sure and steadfast.*

HEBREWS 6:19

 For most people, hope is a "cross-my-fingers" kind of thing shot through with guesswork. But for the believer, hope is *divinely assured things that aren't here yet!*

Our hope is grounded in unshakable promises. While I may misunderstand God's timing or God's ways, and even wonder about God's presence, He doesn't change: "It is impossible for God to lie . . . [thus we] have fled for refuge to lay hold of the hope set before us. This hope we have as an anchor of the soul, both sure and steadfast" (Heb. 6:18–19).

Moments with Majesty

CHRIST IN YOU!

"Repent, and let every one of you be baptized,
in the name of Jesus Christ . . . and you shall receive
the gift of the Holy Spirit."

ACTS 2:38

The Holy Spirit given here is the same One who brought about the incarnation of Jesus, through Mary in a spiritual sense. Hers was the prototypical pathway to "glory" being "revealed" to "flesh."

Just as the Holy Spirit performed that biological miracle in Mary, He is able to work a spiritual one in you and me to bring Jesus alive *in* and *through* us. He's ready to birth divine life within us when we repent and believe in Jesus Christ. And He is able to grow the life of Jesus within us—His character and His traits. Then, His desire is to flow Christ's power and ministry through us to others! It's the spiritual experience of incarnation—"Christ in you!"

The Power and Blessing

THE WEAPON OF PRAISE

The weapons of our warfare are not carnal but mighty in God for pulling down strongholds.

2 CORINTHIANS 10:4

 Faced with the forces of evil, God's people are not to fear. Our greatest resource of resistance doesn't come from any arsenal known to human wisdom or device. It comes from knowing that the battle is the Lord's. We are never to react from a position of weakness but from one of strength. That strength is found in faithfully remaining at our post of praise.

Our best defense is to do what we should know how to do best: offer praise and glory to the Living God, whose enemies will always flee before His mighty power.

The Heart of Praise

WALKING IN OBEDIENCE

I will walk within my house with a perfect heart.

PSALM 101:2

Perfection isn't a demand, it's a goal—and the essence of walking the pathway toward that objective is keeping a heart open to the Holy Spirit. He will only require obedience of you at those points He has already taught you. But you must keep sensitive to His voice, just as surely as you must walk obediently to His counsel.

Responsibility means "your ability to respond," and where your understanding has been enlightened, your bondage to the past broken, and your commitment fully declared, He will expect you to walk as a child of the light.

They way to do so is to know the heart of God through His Word.

Rebuilding the Real You

GOD IS GOOD

He who has seen Me has seen the Father.

JOHN 14:9

 The image of a frowning God, brooding in anger and perched on high ready to hurl a quiver of lightning bolts at the unsuspecting and the helpless is pure fiction. The goodness and beauty of the Father's personality was so perfectly mirrored in Jesus that, the Savior declares, "If you've seen me, you've seen the Father."

The combination of His compassion for the victims of human failure and His triumph over each dilemma surrendered to Him furnishes us with a stamp of God's image: God is loving. God is good. God does good. He cannot even be tempted to do otherwise (James 1:13).

Prayer Is Invading the Impossible

THE SUBMITTED LIFE

It is no longer I who live, but Christ lives in me.

GALATIANS 2:19

Our Savior is the model of the submitted life. And yet He functions with more dynamic authority and dominion than anyone in all history. Look at Him.

He stoops to a manger on earth, though rightfully the King of the Universe.

He accepts rejection without retaliating in kind.

He prays, "Father, not My will, but Yours be done."

He accepts the slashing and spearing of His body, and says, "Father, forgive them, they don't understand."

He calls us to learn the spirit of submission, to let a grander power manifest through us—the power of love.

The Power and Blessing

WELCOME TO THE THRONE

Let us therefore come boldly
to the throne of grace, that we may obtain mercy,
and find grace to help in time of need.

HEBREWS 4:16

"In time of need." That's the time we're most encouraged to come before God's throne. Yet when need arises—and is compounded by our own sense of sin and failure—that's the time we're least inclined to come boldly.

But it's the time we're most invited!

Has your desire to pray been blocked by a sense of guilt?

Be done with that blockade!

Let the truth about the blood of Jesus and the truth about the Father's mercy set you free!

Come boldly. You are welcome in the throne room of heaven.

Prayer Is Invading the Impossible

ON THE STRETCH FOR GOD

Grow in the grace and knowledge
of our Lord and Savior Jesus Christ.

2 PETER 3:18

Jesus is constantly stretching me. You, too?

Of course, you, too. And it's enough to make you sometimes wonder what kind of a bargain you got when you gave your life over to this Man. He is so convinced of His capacity to make us people of large purpose, genuine significance, and high destiny that He keeps on leading us forward.

E. M. Bounds had words for it when he often used the expression, "We must always be on the stretch for God." It's not a rack of torture, but it certainly is a path of growth.

But whatever the demand there are resources, because Jesus is here . . . right now. When this sheep named Jack is accompanied by his Great Shepherd, the whole meadow lights up.

Moments with Majesty

ULTIMATE DELIVERANCE

*Weeping may endure for
a night, but joy comes in the morning.*

PSALM 30:5

Because of the Cross, there is nothing we struggle with that is without either a purpose or an end.

No struggle need ever again be pointless.

No suffering need ever again be unending.

We never face any assault of flesh, devil, circumstances, or personal weakness, but that God's hand is present, mighty, and available to work through it all and beyond it all. This doesn't mean God has planned every bad thing that happens to people. Evil things that are initiated by hell's hatefulness or by human sin, failure, and rebellion create their own problems. But beyond them all, God's ultimate deliverance is our promised inheritance.

How to Live Through a Bad Day

A DREAM COME TRUE

Your will be done on earth as it is in heaven.

MATTHEW 6:10

God has an idea, determines His will, and then brings it to pass. In teaching us to move after the pattern of His workings, He begins by giving us His idea. We receive it as a dream. His Holy Spirit impresses us with the confirming certainty that this idea is His will. And as soon as an idea from God is known to be the will of God, His Word tells us exactly what to do. Pray: "Your will be done on earth as it is in heaven."

From that time on, what you know He sees as an already-accomplished fact begins more and more to appear to you in the same condition. Done. A dream come true. And praise follows on the heels of prayer.

Dream on!

Moments with Majesty

October

LET YOUR

LOVE AND JOY

SO GLORIOUS

SETTLE O'ER US,

GO BEFORE US.

GLORY ON YOUR HOUSE

You will be saved, you and your household.

ACTS 16:31

Families and relationships involve far more than biological genetics. There are spiritual genetics, too. God's promise of glory on your house is a promise with real and practical possibilities—that spiritual life power may be transmitted through your family as surely as hair color. He simply calls us to believe. "You will be saved, you and your household."

In the same way, He also wants to pour out His Spirit on your sons and daughters (Joel 2:28). God wants to bless all those relationships that come within the circle of your home or family life (Exod. 12:4). This is His glory on your house.

Glory on Your House

GOD REBUILDS

*Restore to me the joy of Your
salvation, and uphold me by Your generous Spirit.*

PSALM 51:12

God's purpose in pouring His holiness
toward us through His Son and by His Spirit, is
to save us—

to *restore* all that has been eaten away by the
locusts of sin;

to *refill* all that has been eroded by the streams
of unrighteousness;

to *rebuild* all that has been broken down by
the destructiveness of hell's operations;

to *recover* all that has been decayed by the
works of the flesh.

A Passion for Fullness

GUARD YOUR HEART

*Keep your heart with
all diligence, for out of it spring the issues of life.*

PROVERBS 4:23

There is no more intricate or crucial part of the human makeup than that part of the personality we call the "heart." The importance of our spiritual heart to our health and survival is parallel to the importance of our physical heart.

The Bible tells us that we need to be sensitive, guarding our heart attitudes (Prov. 4:32). We must remember that God judges us in view of what's in our hearts (1 Sam. 16:7), and that wisdom and revelation are the keys to gaining an understanding heart (Eph. 1:17).

God is searching for people whose hearts desire Him and His ways.

Our Daily Walk

BOW AND WORSHIP

Oh come, let us worship and
bow down; let us kneel before the LORD our Maker.

PSALM 95:6

Psalm 95, in calling us to worship, says nothing about our rights. Instead, it summarily calls us to bow down, to kneel before this One whose creatures we are, sheep of His pasture. And make no mistake—the call to bowing and kneeling is more than mere bodily postures. It focuses on the surrender of our will. It means we are granting supreme authority to God. In our worship and in our lives we are giving up our will in favor of His.

To grow in praise and worship is to discover new dimensions of saying to God, *Not my will but Yours be done.*

The Heart of Praise

A MEASURE OF FAITH

God has dealt to each one a measure of faith.

ROMANS 12:3

Dreams are not rare. They fill our hearts and occupy our minds. God puts them there— that is, the ones that really count. Those longings, aspirations, and goals are God-given. That's why He also breathes hope into our hearts to keep us targeted on the good and great things He wants to do if we'll enter into partnership with Him.

Here's where faith comes in. The Bible says that everyone has a measure of faith. This doesn't mean that everyone's faith is perfect, accurate, or functional. But it's there, waiting to be pointed in the right direction and applied in the right way.

Rebuilding the Real You

TWO SIDES TO PRAYER

I give you the authority . . .
over all the power of the enemy.

LUKE 10:19

No one in history manifested more love than Jesus. He patiently ministered with compassion to crowds of sick and tormented people. He labored to the point of exhaustion to relieve human need. . . . But there is another side.

He was furious with religious bigotry that would rather see a man remain deformed than violate tradition. His hand brandished a whip as He rejected religious commercialism.

To see both sides of Jesus is to see both sides of prayer. It is to see the need for compassion and weeping with those who weep. And it is to enter into unabashed warfare when we see the adversary's program violating territory that is rightfully Christ's.

Prayer Is Invading the Impossible

THE PLACE OF HIS LOVE

God is love, and he who abides
in love abides in God, and God in him.

1 JOHN 4:16

The Cross of Christ is the solid foundation for all faith. It is the fountain from which any passion for "more of Him" must begin.

Here is the place we find His love for us. Here is where we affirm the same for one another.

Whatever varied points we may represent on the spectrum of God's Church, here—at the Cross—is the place His completed work of salvation does more than provide grounds for mutual acknowledgment—it demands it. He has bought each of us with His blood. He has birthed us into one family. He has made us brothers and sisters—in Him.

A Passion for Fullness

HIS LIFE, HIS LOVE

All Scripture is given by inspiration of God,
and is profitable for doctrine, for reproof, for correction,
for instruction in righteousness,
that the man of God may be complete,
thoroughly equipped for every good work.

2 TIMOTHY 3:16–17

Jesus has left none of us on earth at the mercy of circumstances or the powers of hell. As members of His Body, the Church is filled with Jesus Himself. We are equipped to introduce His life, His love, and His power into each situation the Holy Spirit brings us to. We have not been left on the defensive or called to preserve the status quo, but equipped to let Jesus happen through us. This brings the enjoyment of a happy partnership in His ongoing victory as His glory flows through us, touching people and circumstances with His life.

Glory on Your House

AUTHOR OF SALVATION

*Having been perfected, He became
the author of eternal salvation to all who obey Him.*

HEBREWS 5:9

Christ has "authored" our salvation. The message He authors is not only one of forgiveness and eternal life provided through His death. It is also a message of relief for the pressure points of suffering.

It's as though Scripture is saying, "The Savior not only saves you from sin, He understands you as a person. He has come to provide the way through your suffering, just as surely as He has provided a way for your release from sin and its power. Come to Jesus, the author of eternal salvation. Since He 'wrote the book,' He understands every dimension and nuance of pain and suffering, and He alone has an answer to it all."

The Visitor

ABUNDANT GENEROSITY

Command those who are rich . . . not to . . .
trust in uncertain riches. . . . Let them do good,
that they be rich in good works.

1 TIMOTHY 6:17–18

God never said His people would not have money. He never said His people would not own property. He never said His people couldn't have fine cars and clothes.

By the same token, neither did He say the verification of their faith would ever be in having material comforts. He hasn't ordained us to prosperity with an eye to our spending our lives wallowing in the gravy of abundance. Instead, He wants us to learn His ways of prosperity so His abundance can be entrusted to us. He does this so we can distribute it all the more abundantly, to be His hand of provision to others in need, whether that need is for His life, His love, or His possession in material circumstances.

The Key to Everything

THE HOLY PLACE

*O, God, You are more awesome than Your
holy places. The God of Israel is He who gives
strength and power to His people.*

PSALM 68:35

God calls us to worship, and there He
wants to display His might. He knows we will face
tasks in which we need to act mightily, and He
wants to supplant our unholiness with His
holiness, our unwholeness with His wholeness.
He is not disposed to frighten us to death for
entering His presence, but to awe us to *life* because
we have been in His presence.

The Ground of All Being wants us to be able
to stand our ground in life's trials. To do so in the
face of sorrow, temptation, illness, and
disappointment requires frequent visits to the holy
place—where God waits to fill us with Himself.

The Heart of Praise

GREATER WORKS

"You will see greater things than these."

JOHN 1:50

We who walk with God into tomorrow need open and obedient hearts—hearts that seek His will, hearts that welcome His mighty works. Our obedience will allow Him to manifest His mightiness in our life situations in varied and dynamic ways!

Make no mistake, dear one. Possessing tomorrow calls for growth beyond our present experience of God's grace. Those new dimensions are to be possessed by us in order that others may know the abundant fruit of His miracle works through us. The divine desire for "greater works" is in the interest of others.

God wants to enlarge our inheritance that we might share it with others.

Taking Hold of Tomorrow

TOUCHING THE ALMIGHTY

Your will be done on earth.

MATTHEW 6:10

God seeks people who will learn to walk with Him and discover how much is possible when faith touches hands with the Almighty. When we see this, we can begin to believe that our praying for His will to be done on earth is actually possible! We will see that it is both our privilege and our responsibility to pray in this way, knowing that when we do so our prayers will be effective.

Our Daily Walk

LARGER THAN LIFE

*I pray, LORD God of heaven, O great
and awesome God . . . let Your ear be attentive . . .
that You may hear the prayer of Your servant.*

NEHEMIAH 1:5–6

God doesn't need to be reminded of His greatness, *we* do. So beginning prayer with praise is neither to cultivate a theology nor to affect a certain abject humility, as though God wanted to be certain we were sufficiently impressed or intimidated by Him.

Instead, praise exalts His greatness and calls my attention to my own limits—personally or circumstantially. Viewing and extolling the enormity of our Father can quickly settle the issue of our confidence. Suddenly, we're standing in renewed amazement at His sufficiency to handle our need!

Because He is *larger* than life, He can handle everything about life!

Rebuilding the Real You

BREAD OF LIFE

"I am the bread which came down from heaven."

JOHN 6:41

 Forever honored as the town where our Savior was born, Bethlehem was so named because it was a center of wheat and meal production—crucially important to nourishing and sustaining the people of ancient Israel.

How poetic and prophetic that God's Son—the Bread of Life—would enter this world at a site named "House of Bread!"

Come . . . and Behold Him!

KNOWN PERSONALLY

*LORD, You have searched me and
known me. You know my sitting down and my rising up.*

PSALM 139:1–2

God's Word never suggests we are to live on secondhand experiences. I may be taught, cared for, and nourished by the help and counsel of others—my mentors as well as my peers—but the One who saved me *for* Himself, and has called me *unto* Himself, also desires to draw me closer *to* Himself.

He is the One who "knows my sitting down and my rising up," who knows "the thoughts and intents" of my heart, who "knows each word before it is spoken from my lips" and who "numbers the hairs of my head." God does more than take statistical notice of my existence. He desires to be personally involved with the details of my life—continually.

Pastors of Promise

SAFE AND SECURE

We have peace with God through our Lord Jesus Christ.

ROMANS 5:1

When the quiet of your soul is assaulted, the ultimate point of refuge is your relationship with the Father. In Jesus' name we have been joined together with the heart of God. And He whose heart reached down to us in Christ has been knit together with us through Christ!

We not only have a Savior who calms the storms of life, but in Christ we "have an anchor" that securely positions us permanently in a safe harbor (Heb. 6:19).

Living and Praying in Jesus' Name

DIVINE MERCY

*"Assuredly, I say to you, today
you will be with Me in Paradise."*

LUKE 23:43

Jesus' response to the thief on the Cross is a study in divine mercy, in grace's readiness to give salvation, in God's immeasurable gentleness toward all who come to Him, and in the truth that it is never too late to seek God. It is a scenario that jangles the nerves of the religionist who would haltingly dispense salvation. It is as dramatic a statement that God's Son could make to say, "Those who come to Me, I will never turn away."

How to Live Through a Bad Day

SEEK HIM

You will seek Me and find Me,
when you search for Me with all your heart.

JEREMIAH 29:13

God wants to reveal Himself to us. He does not want to remain mysterious or unknowable. He wants us to experience His strength, His grace, the provision of His goodness, and His faithfulness. He wants us to know Him in a continually deepening way. But to do so we must come with open, teachable, and hungry hearts.

Jeremiah 29:13 tells us that if we truly seek God with all our hearts, we will find Him. This is neither a mystical nor a mental pursuit. To seek with the heart is to commit our will and affections to wanting Him, to open our minds to the Word of Truth, which teaches us of Him.

Grounds for Living

A BIRTH DAY BLESSING

You formed my inward parts;
You covered me in my mother's womb.

PSALM 139:13

Father-God is the one who planned for you and me. He's the Parent who is eternally committed to fulfill His purpose in us, and to give all grace and power from day to day that His plan for us may be fulfilled.

And birthdays? They ought to be an annual celebration of God's plan for you . . . a new opportunity to declare His blessing upon you for another year.

Let's make a big deal out of these worthy celebrations. Let's take time to give cards and presents and notes and words and greetings . . . and certainly a hug or two! The Lord has created every one of us with magnificent purpose and infinite worth.

Moments with Majesty

WILLING AND AVAILABLE

He who overcomes, I will make him a pillar
in the temple of My God, and he shall go out no more.

REVELATION 3:12

Jesus is saying, "I'm going to take the raw material of your life and shape it. But if you fear something's lacking that might hinder My finishing—don't be afraid. I can create things in you that are now nonexistent!"

Of equal encouragement is the future tense of the Greek verb, *poieo,* which translates literally, "I will keep on making, creating, shaping, and bringing into being, until the project is done!" It's God's way of saying, "I've got the will and the power if you've got the willingness and the availability."

The Power and Blessing

WORSHIPFUL PRAYER

Those who know Your name will put their trust in You.

PSALM 9:10

☀ Let us approach God with a prayer of confession, acknowledging our sins and imperfection and our longing to partake of His holiness.

In prayer our speech also includes intercession and supplication. There's never a shortage of situations needing God's intervention. So we intercede—being bold enough to ask Him to step into the middle of our muddle!

Finally, our worshipful praying includes exaltation and adoration. We magnify Him who is worthy above all others and adore Him simply because of who He is.

The Heart of Praise

ETERNAL FLAME OF PRAISE

*Let us continually offer the sacrifice of praise to God,
that is, the fruit of our lips, giving thanks to His name.*

HEBREWS 13:15

Notice the word *continually*. Keep the flame of praise burning in your life continually. Ceaselessly. In all circumstances.

I'm not suggesting that you get in some private cubicle in a monastic corner of the universe where you repeat formula praises every waking hour.

I believe the Lord is simply saying, "Whatever you do, whether you're changing your clothes or taking out the trash or driving along the freeway, just keep the flame burning. Be a person who praises. Keep an attitude of praise. Never let the flame die out."

Moments with Majesty

ASK WITH BOLDNESS

Ask, and it will be given to you.

MATTHEW 7:7

In this verse Jesus is saying, "Your first barrier isn't God—it's your own hesitance to ask freely. You need to learn the kind of boldness that isn't afraid to ask—whatever the need or circumstance."

It isn't the brashness of a smart aleck making demands, but the forwardness of a person who is so taken with such an awareness of personal need that he abandons normal protocol.

Ask with unabashed forwardness. Ask with shameless boldness!

Prayer Is Invading the Impossible

VOICE OF GOD

When You said, "Seek My face,"
my heart said to You, "Your Face, LORD, I will seek."

PSALM 27:8

Can you picture what the psalmist is saying? The Holy Spirit spoke to a person's heart, the person recognized it and wrote in response: "Lord, what You're saying to me by Your Spirit, I'm saying back right now. I'm going to do it."

I recently came across this thought: "Spirituality is the sum of our responses to what we believe to be the voice of God." That's a great definition of spiritual growth—tuning our hearts to what the Lord says and responding on His terms.

You'll find it happens best when you have sufficient time alone with Him to hear His voice, to record His words to you, and to live as His Holy Spirit directs you.

The Power and Blessing

DOORWAY OF PRAYER

Draw near to God and He will draw near to you.

JAMES 4:8

Prayer opens the doorway to the dynamic that shakes, shatters, and does violence to the world of darkness. Hell's force holds no respect for our attempts to match its wit or its workings. It is forced to yield ground to those believers who pray until they receive power.

Prayer can change anything. The impossible doesn't exist.

God's is the power.

Ours is the prayer.

Without Him, we cannot.

Without us, He will not.

Prayer Is Invading the Impossible

CONFIDENCE IN HIS NAME

These signs will follow those who believe:
In My name they will cast out demons; . . . they will
lay hands on the sick, and they will recover.

MARK 16:17–18

Let the name of Jesus stir new confidence in your life today. He has granted His own name as the signature, the badge of authority, the security, the guarantee of every promise offered in God's Word. And in that name, we are to expect results—in our life, in our family, in our neighborhood, in our church, and in our world.

Yes there is the waiting of faith and the patience of hope, but people who pray in Jesus' name can expect action. Boldly believe!

Moments with Majesty

BLESSED ARE THE FLEXIBLE

Behold, I make all things new.

REVELATION 21:5

Throughout my years of walking with Jesus, I've discovered He keeps me in a permanent state of transition. And I've learned a little about the potential for joy when you allow the Holy Spirit to keep "flex" in your soul.

I don't want to become stodgy, unshapeable, or inflexible. The ongoing working of the Spirit in my life—and yours—will keep us "hanging loose."

Someone reminded me of those things just the other day. "Blessed are the flexible," my friend said, "for verily, they shall not be broken."

Moments with Majesty

KINSMAN REDEEMER

*He humbled Himself and became obedient
to the point of death, even the death of the cross.*

PHILIPPIANS 2:8

When Jesus came to earth, He came at unimaginable expense to Himself.

Jesus knew He was God, knew He possessed the infinite resources of heaven at His fingertips, but He laid it all down. He emptied Himself. He made Himself of "no reputation." When He stepped into human flesh, He poured out all of His prerogatives as God, choosing to be completely and totally human.

He lived and suffered and died in a normal human body.

He did it so He might become our kinsman-redeemer.

A New Time and Place

WE ARE BLESSED

God so loved the world that He gave His only begotten Son, that whoever believes in Him should not perish but have everlasting life.

JOHN 3:16

God's Son allowed Himself to be sown as a seed buried in death, that the great harvest of our souls might be gathered unto eternal life.

Let's lift our voices. We are:

People who are blessed by the abundance of God's hand.

People who have received love and grace beyond measure.

People redeemed to eternal life through Jesus Christ our Lord.

Moments with Majesty

BLESSING AND STRUGGLE

Father, if it is Your will, take this cup away
from Me; nevertheless not My will, but Yours, be done.

LUKE 22:41

Nothing happens for our blessing without a struggle. To understand that, we need to look at the Cross. Not even God could redeem us without His own suffering and death.

In Gethsemane Jesus pled: "If it be possible, let this cup pass from me." He was asking if there was anything in the eternal order of things that would allow for an adjusted pathway of delivering mankind from destruction. But His perfect humanity continued, "Nevertheless not My will, but Yours, be done."

He settled on what He knew to be the divine order: Without the shedding of blood there is no remission of sins. God invites us to bring our struggles and fears to Him, even as we accept His will.

Prayer Is Invading the Impossible

November

CHRIST IS KING,

EVER SING,

OF LIFE

OVERFLOWING.

GOD'S GREATNESS

As for the Almighty, we cannot find Him;
He is excellent in power, in judgment and abundant
justice; He does not oppress.

JOB 37:23

God is not manlike, not even supermanlike. He clearly states that He is wholly "other" from us—on another plane entirely. And though that should humble us, He doesn't say it to humiliate us. Nor does He declare His exceeding difference from us to make us grovel before His throne. But we must see something of these dimensions of His greatness to fully appreciate the investment He makes in visiting us. Here is the Eternal One planning to give us time; the Omniscient One preparing to confine Himself to one place; and the Omniscient One who, knowing all things, still comes to learn of life on the terms of His own creation.

The Visitor

True Happiness

Rejoice in the Lord always. Again I will say, rejoice!

PHILIPPIANS 4:4

Yes, we are a happy people. But this is not a happiness that skips like a flat rock across the surface of pleasant situations. This is not happiness tied like a kite-tail to feelings that change with the wind. This true happiness derives from the joy of the Lord—an artesian fountain that cannot be stopped by man or demon. God's Holy Spirit pours it forth, so let us live in its fullness.

And again I say, *rejoice!*

Come . . . and Behold Him!

LIVE FORGIVINGLY

Put on tender mercies, . . . forgiving one another.

COLOSSIANS 3:12–13

Don't forget to forgive! Don't return to joyless living by becoming a forgetful servant. You have been forgiven. Now live forgivingly. Give up your claim to being "right." Give over your burden of bitterness to God. Give in to the Holy Spirit's correction when tempted not to forgive.

Forgiving keeps the soul and body healthy.

Forgiving allows a reconciled relationship.

Forgiving maintains gratitude for God's grace.

The Key to Everything

A Meal to Celebrate!

"This is My body which is given
for you; do this in remembrance of Me."

"This is My body," Jesus said, as He broke the unleavened bread at the Last Supper. For us, the term *body* recalls both the physical body of Christ that was broken on the Cross and the Church, "which is His Body" (Eph. 1:22).

Let us also remember Jesus' words, "This is my blood." In the wine of communion we participate with each other and with our Lord in the very essence of that which saves us—the blood of Jesus Christ.

What outbursts of praise this should call forth! Let's never allow the Lord's Supper to degenerate into a morbid memory, a full routine, or a rote ritual. Here is the meal we share with Him who delivered us from bondage!

The Heart of Praise

GROW IN CHRIST

*Grow in the grace and knowledge
of our Lord and Saviour Jesus Christ.*

2 PETER 3:18

God beckons us to a life of ceaselessly stretched potential.

He wants to enlarge the horizons of our vision.

He opens the vistas of a tomorrow filled with high destiny.

This is what growth in Christ is about: Growth is more than merely acquiring a body of information through study. It involves a steady advancement in *applying* the truth. Growth is never becoming so secure or comfortable in past victories that we become unavailable to move toward new challenges and broader horizons.

Jesus' is calling us all unto broader realms— to the tomorrows He has planned for us! They're worth exploring. And they're worth possessing!

Taking Hold of Tomorrow

CALVARY'S LOVE

*Submit to God. Resist the
devil and he will flee from you.*

JAMES 4:7

The ultimate and final victory obtained at Calvary is about God's love for us. When the hearts of His redeemed are filled with that love, there is no power of hell able to withstand it.

In every sense, Calvary broke the serpent's back. The Cross holds the ultimate declaration of victory: "It is finished."

Yet the outworking of this power is possible only as we learn to apply Calvary's love.

Prayer Is Invading the Impossible

LIVING WATER

He who believes in Me, as the Scripture
has said, out of his heart will flow rivers of living water.

JOHN 7:38

True holiness is not the result of human efforts or enforced works of holy living. The power of holy living simply flows from a lifestyle that keeps our human conduits uncluttered by carnality and untainted by sin. God's love and power simply happen, as rivers of living water flow to fill ordinary believers, and overflow with pure hope and health to those they meet.

Nothing could be less religious or forced than this. Nothing could be more beautiful or blessed. Full holiness rises with holy fullness.

A Passion for Fullness

GOD'S FULL OFFER

Because I live, you will live also.

JOHN 14:19

When Jesus said, "Because I live, you will live also," He was declaring a new dimension of life available to all who receive Him.

Most believers in Jesus live an inferior quality of life simply because they've never come to terms with His full offer. Christ the Lord, the resurrected Son of God, has made available to us both forgiveness of sins and fullness of life. Forgiveness comes when we receive Him as Savior. Fullness comes when we receive the offer of life in the glory of His power.

Glorious Morning!

GODLY, NOT RELIGIOUS

You have made known to me the ways of life.

ACTS 2:28

Jesus possessed balance.

He was the ultimate saint, but He mixed with notorious sinners.

He was at times the most sensitive respondent, while at other times He was the boldest initiator.

Once He shouted aloud in the Temple courtyard; later He knelt silently at the same place to write with His finger in the dust.

Jesus was everything of humanity and nothing of superficiality; everything of godliness and nothing of religiosity.

Glory on Your House

PAID IN FULL

No one takes [My life]
from me, but I lay it down of Myself.

JOHN 10:18

In dying, Jesus affirms His full devotion to us. He wasn't forced to die; He chose to die for us.

Now that transaction is accomplished. The price has been fully paid.

I can stand before God with assurance, for my sin has been swept aside; it has been disannulled.

By the power of Christ's conclusive sacrifice—once for all—my conscience is washed free of sin's guilt and shame. He's alive and I'm forgiven!

The Visitor

LET YOUR LIGHT SHINE

Let your light so shine before men, that they may
see your good works and glorify your Father in heaven.

MATTHEW 5:16

No heavenly law dictates that we sell everything we have, cloister ourselves in a commune, and live on organically grown vegetables and goat's milk. That's been done in forced ways, and it doesn't work. Forced ways never work because that is not how God does things. Rather, He calls us to be salt and light in the world, and much of what "shines" through us of His light will be in the way we handle the everyday, ordinary things of life.

His spirit of loving, giving, and sharing among and through His people is one of God's primary means for "lighting" the world.

The Key to Everything

PUT GOD FIRST

*In everything you do, put God first, and he
will direct you and crown your efforts with success.*

PROVERBS 3:5–7, TLB

In everything you do, put God first. Take time in counsel with the Lord. Let Him help you outline the basic tasks and responsibilities your day holds. As you do this, your day will be more orderly. Whatever you put in the Lord's hands will always return with His blessing.

He will direct you. This is God's promise, and He will keep it. Through this verse He is saying, "If you acknowledge Me, I'll take control of your day in a way that will assist and profit you." He will lead us through every detail of each day to its highest fulfillment.

Our Daily Walk

COME TO THE FATHER

When he was still a great way off,
his father saw him and had compassion, and ran
and fell on his neck and kissed him.

LUKE 15:20

No matter your weakness or failure, never hesitate to come to our awesome Father God. Borrow from His divine strength, and then honor and praise the source of that strength. Let's be taught by the parable of the prodigal son. Not only is the forgiving love of the Father taught there, but it's also about a son who, having flouted his disregard for his father at first, later remembers and acknowledges the source of his security.

The return to his home was wonderful, but more awesome than the place was the person who welcomed him—his father. As the prodigal came to his earthly father, so we are invited to come to our heavenly Father.

The Heart of Praise

GOD'S LAWS WORK

*He who heeds the word wisely will
find good, and whoever trusts in the LORD, happy is he.*

PROVERBS 16:20

There are no mysteries to knowing how life works.

God has revealed the ways of wisdom pertaining to every issue of life in His Word.

As natural laws govern mathematics or physics, so God's laws work when applied to our families, our jobs, our finances, and our future.

God's Word provides practical instruction for victorious daily living. His precepts and principles are the "owner's manual" to the life He's given us. God's laws are not given so we can earn our way to heaven. He's provided them to make life work.

Taking Hold of Tomorrow

INTIMACY AND POWER

O God, You are my God; early will I seek You.

PSALM 63:1

 There is a pathway of power available to every believer who wants his life to grow to its fullest dimension in Christ.

That pathway begins with spending personal, intimate time with God. His deepest workings in our lives—those that will shape us into His image—will take place when we are alone with Him, keeping closely and personally related in His presence.

Our Daily Walk

GOD PLANNED YOU!

Your eyes saw my substance, being yet
unformed. And in Your book they all were written.

PSALM 139:16

Every person is a case of *planned parenthood*—God planned you! Whatever else may have seemed to be happenstance, there were no surprises in heaven when either you or I arrived on earth!

Because some were born outside of marriage, with less than perfect bodies, or conceived in less than desired circumstances, people draw the conclusion that God wasn't involved in the process. But listen: The fact that God may not have willed the way a person came into the world, does not mean He has not planned a *purpose* for that individual. Long before anyone is conceived, God's purpose for that life is foreseen.

Moments with Majesty

THE HEART OF GOD

He became their Savior. . . .
In His love and in His pity He redeemed them.

ISAIAH 63:9

God doesn't need "more to do." After all, He has a universe to administer. He has places to go and things to do. He has legions of angels flashing through the cosmos at the speed of thought doing His bidding on missions our minds can't even conceive. But wonder of wonders, He not only stepped down to our dust-speck planet to save us from our sins and the sentence of death, He continually steps into our lives as Redeemer. He continues to hear and respond when we cry out to Him from the quicksand of our circumstances.

He redeems because it is in the great heart of God to redeem.

A New Time and Place

WALK IN HIS LIGHT

Then God said, "Let there be light."

GENESIS 1:3

In the same sense that God "spoke" and light rushed forth to bring a new world with new growth, God still speaks "light" into the confusion and darkness of our daily circumstances. He is instantly at hand to show the way, to lead us in His light, to defuse the darkness around us.

His presence shines! Where He is, there is light—simply because He is there. To walk in Jesus is to walk in His light.

Living and Praying in Jesus' Name

CRY OUT TO GOD

*You, O LORD, do not be far
from Me; O My Strength, hasten to help Me!*

PSALM 22:19

The cry of the psalmist is in the spirit of privileged candor that God welcomes from those who worship Him. In response, He promises two things: (1) your cry will never fall on deaf ears, and (2) time will always bring an answer in your best interests. Always.

When "bad day blues" turn black with the unanswerable, and everything you thought you knew backfires, forget human philosophies or riddling theologies. Cry out to God. He doesn't mind your complaints, and He's never far away.

How to Live Through a Bad Day

INCREDIBLE TREASURE

I know the thoughts that I think toward you,
says the LORD, . . . to give you a future and a hope.

JEREMIAH 29:11

Every person on earth is a special part of God's creation, endowed by Him with unique purpose and destiny.

Every person is beloved by Him, even before we understand our sin, our need, or being lost outside of Christ. The Creator hears the cry of every one of His creatures and shows mercy to all.

The Father gave us life and the incredible treasure of what He made us to be. He gave us His Son in order to retrieve that treasure, and the instant we yield our lives to Him, He gives us the kind of life that not only transforms us now but provides assurance of eternity with Him forever.

Grounds for Living

GOD IS OUR "ABBA"

*If you . . . know how to give good gifts to
your children, how much more will your heavenly
Father give the Holy Spirit to those who ask Him!*

LUKE 11:13

As our heavenly Father, God delights in
His children who pursue Him with passion,
persistence, obedience, and worship. He responds
not merely to our emotions or reasoning, but out
of the intimacy of our *relationship* with Him. We
may not only call Him "Father," we may call Him
"Abba" (Hebrew for *daddy*). It is because we have
chosen to align our will with His that we
enjoy this personal relationship, only to
discover that it leads us to praying for
what He longs to do anyway.

Rebuilding the Real You

POWER AND BLESSING

The eyes of your understanding being enlightened;
that you may know what is the hope of His calling.

EPHESIANS 1:18

The contrast between what we see ourselves to be and what God's Spirit promises we will be is like blinding sunlight striking the eyes as the shades of a darkened room are suddenly raised. But the power and blessing of God are intended for you!

That's *power*—the power of God both birthing and bringing about. It's God at work in human clay, shaping, molding, and fashioning until the earthdust of our humanity becomes a treasure chest of divine wealth.

That's *blessing*—the joy of experiencing God's unfolding purpose in your life. We are moved to rise in praise when the high moments come and to stand firm when tears mark the path forward. There's a name for this process. It's called *discipleship*.

The Power and Blessing

WORSHIP AND THE WORD

Speak, LORD, for Your servant hears.

1 SAMUEL 3:9

It is impossible to worship God acceptably and not come to Him in right relationship to His statutes—the Word of God. It is folly to suppose that we can come to Him in worship if in our spirits there is a tendency to disobey what the Bible says.

True worship is never separate from the Word. We hear the Word of grace that comes to us as coals from the altar on which Christ gave Himself for us, burning away our misunderstandings and inadequate knowledge.

And hearing that Word of forgiveness for our sin and failures makes us want to worship and praise Him even more and to say, "Speak, Lord, Your servant is listening. Command, and I will obey."

The Heart of Praise

DEEP DOWN GLADNESS

Because He is at my
right hand . . . my heart is glad.

PSALM 16:8–9

If you'll allow the Holy Spirit to, He will enable you to receive God's precious Word with faith, hope, obedience—and with joy. The joy He brings is not only personal down deep in your soul, but it penetrates your relationships with other brothers and sisters in Christ.

As God's redeemed, walking in His Word and by His Spirit, you can enter tomorrow rejoicing that God's commitment to His purpose in you is absolute. And you can live every day with confidence, assured of the inevitability of His life triumphing in you.

Rebuilding the Real You

ASK AND RECEIVE

Whatever things you ask when you pray,
believe that you receive them, and you will have them.

MARK 11:24

You never need hesitate to ask God for something just because you asked for something else earlier. Any hint that heaven gets too busy with previous requests to have either time or supply for the next is pure folly.

Here's what you need to remember:

1. You have a friend in the Heavenly Father. He's on your side, and available anytime, in every circumstance.

2. Boldness is your privilege. Your assignment is to ask. His commitment is to give—as much as you need.

Prayer Is Invading the Impossible

SUNDAY APPOINTMENT

So He came to Nazareth. . . . And as His custom
was, He went into the synagogue on the Sabbath Day.

LUKE 4:16

I can't help laughing at those who complain about attending church and refuse to go because "the place is too spiritually 'dead'!"

You want to argue about that with Jesus? Go ahead!

"Well Lord, You certainly know things aren't as spiritual over there as they ought to be. You know those people at church aren't warm and friendly."

And Jesus replies: "Warm and friendly? Have you ever been to Nazareth? The day I was there they tried to throw Me off the cliff!"

But Jesus showed up at the synagogue anyway . . . "as His custom was."

The Power and Blessing

KEEP ON ASKING

Everyone who asks receives, and he who seeks finds.

MATTHEW 7:8

God's will is that we seek Him. "Ask, and keep on asking," Jesus tells His disciples. The hearing heart and all-wise mind of Father God are not components in some heavenly computer that might blow a fuse if we ask too much or too often. Heaven's storehouse is never in short supply, and God isn't rationing answers to prayer. Let's settle it: He's the Creator.

When you're dealing with the Source of all things, nothing is a problem.

Prayer Is Invading the Impossible

AN ENDLESS LIFE

There arises another priest who has come,
. . . according to the power of an endless life.

HEBREWS 7:15–16

I vote for life. I say, LIVE!

But live in the "power of an endless life." What magnificent words! They express the dynamic that Jesus can work in the life of anyone who will let Him.

And He keeps making life bigger!

His vastness dispels small-mindedness, non-expectancy, and fear. He brings wisdom, discernment, and sure footing to the marketplace of daily living. His endless Life in us brings powerful peace.

Moments with Majesty

A LIVING HOPE

Blessed be the God and Father of our Lord Jesus Christ, who . . . has begotten us again to a living hope.

1 PETER 1:3

It is the song of the gospel and the message of the Kingdom of God: "Let the hopeless find hope, let the broken be healed, let the oppressed go free!"

What is it about the Kingdom of God that offers such a promise of breakthrough?

It is not a matter of fortune or luck. It is a matter of love.

It is the way of the King. He reverses situations. He turns impossibilities on their heads. He transforms darkness into dazzling light and plants living hope in the lives of all who come to Him.

A New Time and Place

THE HOLINESS OF GOD

Holy, holy, holy, Lord God Almighty,
who was and is and is to come.

Holiness is that attribute of God by which He preserves the integrity of His own being. That means that God never needs to be reminded to be good, loving, wise, or wonderful. He doesn't labor to accomplish what we define as "being holy."

Because God's very nature is holy, He will never be less than what He is already. His holiness guarantees the changeless integrity of His own being:

He will never be without love for you.

He will never be less than merciful.

He will never be other than just.

His holiness is what preserves the perfection and completeness of His person.

Rebuilding the Real You

December

GOD IS MAN;

ETERNITY CONFINED

TO TIME THAT

MEN MIGHT

BE RENEWED

TO LIVE

IN DIGNITY.

THE JOY OF THE LORD

"Behold, I bring you good tidings of great joy which will be to all people. For there is born to you this day in the city of David a Savior, who is Christ the Lord."

LUKE 2:10–11

Joy is the pulse beat to the heart of the message that has resounded since the birth of Christ:

The news is good: *I bring you good tidings.*

The joy is great: *of great joy.*

The focus is you: *there is born to you.*

The time is now: *this day.*

And God is here: *a Savior, who is Christ the Lord!"*

That joy is God's strength for your soul.

Rebuilding the Real You

DECEMBER 2

GOD GIVES PEACE

*May the Lord of peace Himself
give you peace always in every way.*

2 THESSALONIANS 3:16

There are often unpredictable turns in the road of life. Along the way, we may encounter overwhelming obstacles of conflict, loss, and suffering. But our Lord Jesus has given us His peace to carry us through every troubling, fearful situation (John 14:27).

This is no ordinary peace. It is the peace of Jesus Christ Himself—a peace that is greater than the temporary illusion of calm the world has to offer. It is the peace that surpasses all understanding (Phil. 4:7).

Living and Praying in Jesus' Name

SEASONAL REMINDERS

Splendor and majesty are
before him; strength and joy in his dwelling place.

1 CHRONICLES 16:27, NIV

Decorating the house at Christmas in neither a surrender to pagan traditions nor a capitulation to commercialism. Listen . . .

if God commissioned angels to roll back the night and fill it with blazing light,

if God provided a celestial choir to serenade a few startled shepherds and graced the heavens with a miracle star,

if God went to all this trouble to open our eyes to His entry into our world, then we needn't apologize for festooning our home with a few seasonal reminders!

Come . . . and Behold Him!

GOD GOES WITH US

*"If Your Presence does not go
with us, do not bring us up from here."*

EXODUS 33:15

Moses had miracles in Egypt and at Sinai.

He had manna every morning.

Water flowed as he struck the rock.

But Moses said, "Lord, beyond all miracles and success, I want *You.*"

If we have the Lord, everything else takes care of itself. He is the One who gives the *promise.* He is the One who gives us the *power* to live in His patterns, principles, and pathways. He is the One whose *presence* will be with us every step of the way.

Taking Hold of Tomorrow

GOD AMONG US

*"Sacrifice and offering You did
not desire, but a body You have prepared for Me."*

HEBREWS 10:5

At one moment, the "body" is hardly a body at all. It is but a cell in the womb of a virgin, in a small city, in a tiny nation, in one small corner of a fallen planet.

In one microsecond, the primal form of the Son disappears from the throne room of heaven, and in that same split-moment, the Holy Spirit places the life of the Second Person of the Godhead within the womb of a maiden.

The inconceivable has been conceived.

The Word will become flesh and God will live and breathe among us.

The Visitor

DIAMONDS OF PRAISE

"They shall be Mine," says the LORD
of hosts, "on the day that I make them My jewels."

MALACHI 3:17

God's Word says there will come a day when you and I will see that our words of praise weren't lost in the air. They are even now being stored up in God's treasury. On that day God will bring out a treasure chest and say, "Look! These jewels, this treasure, is gathered from the words of praise you offered Me while you were on earth. Well done—enter into the joys of your Lord!"

It isn't farfetched to say there are diamonds spilling from your lips with your words of worship. Our praise is a treasury of priceless jewels to the Lord.

The Heart of Praise

MORE THAN MERRY

Blessed be Your glorious name,
which is exalted above all blessing and praise!

NEHEMIAH 9:5

Christmas is more than merely "merry." Christmas is *mighty.* Love and laughter, gifts and giving, trees and tinsel, holly and reindeer, carols and bells, pageantry and celestial music—*all of it*—I mean A-L-L of it—has an inherent potential for mightiness.

The qualifying factor is the presence of the Holy Spirit. When He is present, all the accouterments of Christmas have a tender power that can bless, strengthen, heal, restore, and bring entry into God's broad blessing of salvation.

When He is absent, carols ring hollow. Greetings, wishes, and smiles lie on the surface, like glitter glued on a flat card. Lights and decorations are only so much window dressing. But where the Holy Spirit is, there is power.

Come . . . and Behold Him!

FREELY AND FULLY

He who did not spare His own Son,
but delivered Him up for us all, how shall He not
with Him also freely give us all things.

ROMANS 8:32

The life of God's Son was given so that life for every one of us might be gained—*fully.*

The plan, price, and provision of salvation was finished so that God's plan for each of us could be afforded and received—*freely.*

The hope of new birth and eternal life was started so that any one of us could enter God's kingdom now, and finally, enter heaven—*forever.*

The Cross is the fountainhead of fullness in everything—finding a fulfilled life, a fulfilling future, and an eternity of fulfillment in the presence of the God.

The Key to Everything

THE KING OF KINGS

His life is the light that shines through the darkness.

JOHN 1:5, TLB

Jesus is the central personality of history, and whether Christmas is canned or canonized, packaged in ribbon and sold for profit or sanctified in a cathedral where humble souls worship, He is the inescapable Christ. The fury of opposition to His praise seeks to ban pageantry and sterilize holy celebration to suit the antagonism of organized unbelief.

But Jesus keeps rising again.

Every Christmas turns out to be an Easter.

Jesus Christ is still the King of kings. There's no getting away from it . . . anywhere!

Come . . . and Behold Him!

GOD'S GOOD GIFTS

*Every good gift and every perfect gift is
from above, and comes down from the Father of lights.*

JAMES 1:17

With every gift you purchase, every gift
you wrap, and every gift you place under the tree,
remember this: God has gifts for you, and in
quantities greater than you can dream. These gifts
are infinitely more valuable than the tinsel and
materialistic toys pursued so desperately by the
world. He has gifts of peace, strength, joy,
fulfillment, and significance in life that will draw
you out of bed each morning like a magnet.

He's looking to lavish His gifts upon people
who will come to simple dependence upon His
grace and rest in simple faith upon His greatness.

Come . . . and Behold Him!

GOD'S HONOR

Make a joyful shout to God, all the earth! Sing out the
honor of His name; make His praise glorious.

PSALM 66:1–2

In the Old Testament the word most often translated "glory" is *chabod,* a word that basically refers to "weight" or "substance."

Another meaning of *chabod* is "honor." For example, have you ever been in a courtroom when the judge entered and everyone stood? Or in a room where a head of state drew people to their feet just by making an entrance? These are gestures showing the "weight" we give to the presence of those whom we honor.

So the psalmist sings, "Make a joyful shout to God, all the earth! Sing out the honor *(chabod)* of His name; make His praise glorious *(chabod).*" Does God carry more "weight" with you than anything else in the world?

The Heart of Praise

A LEARNING TIME

*Everyone who has heard and
learned from the Father comes to Me.*

JOHN 6:45

Time in God's presence was never meant to be an *earning* time. Instead, it's a *learning* time.

Prayer is not a "works" program—a legislated system of acquiring merit and, thereby, results. But prayer does enter strongly into the development of my relationship with God, and it isn't because He gets to like me more, but because I get to know Him better. It has to do with knowing the Lord, understanding His heart and ways, and gaining His wisdom to guide and direct my life.

I learn about God before His Throne. And it's in that very setting that I'm also most likely to learn about *me* . . . while I'm with Him.

Rebuilding the Real You

GOD'S GIFT

God did not send His Son
into the world to condemn the world, but that the
world through Him might be saved.

JOHN 3:17

Where is the "merry" in "Merry Christmas"?

Where is the "joy" in "Joy to the World"?

Where is the "happy" in "Happy Holidays"?

Answer: The soaring gladness of Christmas is directly linked to God's gift of Jesus to us and for us.

Apart from that glorious fact, there is no logic to the season's existence, much less for our festive rejoicing. The celebration of Christmas derives its meaning and highest fulfillment from this radiant reality: *God with us!*

Come . . . and Behold Him!

PROVISION AND POWER

This is He who came by water and blood—Jesus Christ.

1 JOHN 5:6

God has poured out His forgiveness through the death of His Son, with blood and water gushing from His wounds to atone for sin and restore the broken bond between God and man.

God has poured out His truth in His Holy Word to bring light to blinded minds and liberty to bound souls, with streams of truth to cleanse away the debris of confusion and to sweep in with eternal wisdom.

God has poured out His Holy Spirit that those rivers of living water may course through the Church like streams through a dam's sluice gates, generating power for vital living, loving service, and dynamic ministry.

A Passion for Fullness

THE GREATEST GIFT

The Word became flesh and dwelt among us.

JOHN 1:14

God . . . a baby!

It is the ultimate vulnerability—God surrendering Himself to become a man. It extends beyond the limits of human imagination, but not beyond human comprehension. Because of the unimaginable I can receive the eternal. Because of the sacrifice the Father made—giving His Beloved—and because of the redemptive price the Son paid—giving His blood—I can be born again.

I am forgiven, transformed, and brought to the Father forever. It is truly the greatest gift of all.

Come . . . and Behold Him!

WONDERFUL WONDERS

*He will be great, and will
be called the Son of the Highest.*

LUKE 1:32

Since the Light of the World has come, lights strung across the roof only shout it from the housetop. Candles and candelabra, stars and starlight, gifts and giving, songs and sonnets, lights and lightheartedness, angel cookies and wise-men ornaments—all are consistent with what transpired on our little planet two thousand years ago.

The Great One was born among us and born one of us! Is it any wonder the echoes of that great visitation roll down through the centuries? God lavishly spread wonders in our midst during the Advent of our Savior. That we celebrate the memory with attention and care, the wonder-filled and wonder-full, is entirely appropriate.

Come . . . and Behold Him!

LOVE, JOY, AND PEACE

You shall know the truth,
and the truth shall make you free.

JOHN 8:32

Jesus had pioneered a new race.

From among the spiritually dead, He has called to Himself all who will join Him in new life. He welcomes everyone to eternal life—made available to mankind when He broke the death trap by succumbing voluntarily to it.

And then rising again.

We are the freed, who have answered His call. And it is His abundant life in us that makes possible our experience of love, joy, and peace.

Prayer Is Invading the Impossible

A PROMISED PROMISE

That by two immutable things, in which it is impossible for God to lie, we might have strong consolation.

HEBREWS 6:18

The writer to the Hebrews explains how God's promise to bless His people includes both His *promise* and His *oath;* "that by two immutable things, in which it is impossible for God to lie" we might find hope.

God underwrites His own "fail-safe" provision. He has promised, and then He sealed His promise with an oath, essentially saying, *"I promise to keep my promise."* God didn't need to reinforce His promise, because it is impossible for Him to lie in the first place! And yet, in His gentle understanding of our fears and fragility of faith, He declared these words of absolute, unshakable assurance.

What love, patience, and grace.

Taking Hold of Tomorrow

THE STAR BEAMS HOPE

Behold, I will again do a marvelous work
among this people, a marvelous work and a wonder.

ISAIAH 29:14

Although no one can make a biblical case
for Christmas trees, we gather around ours with joy.
We see in its living branches a symbol of everlasting
life given us because of Jesus' death on the "tree"
at Calvary.

The lights on our tree gleam a testimony of
His Light-of-the-World glory.

The ornaments reflect the decorative splendor
with which His kindness adorns our lives.

The star beams hope with a heavenward ray,
reminding us that it is from there He shall come
again.

The season is upon us, and in celebrating it
we make it His!

Come . . . and Behold Him!

THE PROSPECT OF PROMISES

*Not one thing has failed of all the
good things which the LORD your God spoke
concerning you. All have come to pass.*

JOSHUA 23:14

Packaged in the Person of Jesus is every gift we will ever need to fulfill every longing we may ever have. It will take a lifetime to unwrap the essentials for our present, and an eternity to unfold the glories for our future.

But start *now*.

Start by letting your heart embrace promises for today and the New Year just ahead. Open His Word and feast on the prospects His eternal covenant opens up to us. The promises of the Bible deliver meaning and hope to the highest of our desires and the deepest of our dilemmas.

Come . . . and Behold Him!

REST FOR THE RAGGED

*Come to Me, all you who labor and
are heavy laden, and I will give you rest.*

MATTHEW 11:28

The Psalms, though great, swelling songs to God, can often be raw and ragged. They are honest-to-life as well as honest-to-God. They give vent to sorrow and anguish as well as to exultation. Some people mistakenly think that life has to be going smoothly in order for them to worship. Not the psalmists! To be sure, they shout and sing with joy. But they also worship when their hearts are burdened with grief. Sometimes their songs are wrenched from their groaning.

Despite any burden or pressure you may have brought to this moment, let me encourage you to open your heart and worship Him who invites you: *"Come to Me, all you who labor and are heavy laden, and I will give you rest."* *The Heart of Praise*

THE SPIRIT OF CHRISTMAS

My spirit has rejoiced in God my Savior.

LUKE 1:47

Jesus lives at our house. And it's His birthday.

He is the Spirit of Christmas—*Holy* is His name. And whether you are thinking of the *Baby* in the manger, the *Child* whose parents escaped with Him into Egypt, the *Teenager* in the temple in Jerusalem, the *Prophet* scattering moneychangers' tables, the *Healer* restoring vision to blind eyes, the *Deliverer* liberating the demoniac, the *Teacher* revealing the truth of the eternal Father, the *Savior* dying upon Calvary, the *Lord* rising from the dead, or *Christ His Majesty* ruling on high at the Father's right hand . . . He's here this Christmas.

Come . . . and Behold Him!

PATTERNS FOR LIFE

*The LORD will perfect that which
concerns me; Your mercy, O LORD, endures forever.*

PSALM 138:8

All of us understand the concept of a pattern or blueprint. The tailor who designed the clothes you're wearing had to follow a pattern or the clothing would not fit. It would be too tight in some places, or it would be too loose and would feel uncomfortable in other places. A building would not be safe, nor would an engine run, if not made according to the blueprint.

The same is true with life. We have to start with a blueprint.

The Bible's patterns for life are not merely religious rules, they're laws that make life work. That is, they're patterns that work so we can live life the way God designed it. His commandments and precepts are blueprints—designs provided so we can build lives that stand strong and tall.

The Key to Everything

JOY TO THE WORLD!

They rejoiced with exceedingly great joy.

MATTHEW 2:10

We rejoice because Joy has come to earth.

We give gifts because the Best and Grandest has been given to us. We feast because the Bread of Life has been provided. We sing carols of endless variety because all of life has been penetrated by The Song.

This Christmas Eve we praise the One

…who came to cleanse and purify our souls through His Cross.

…who came to fill us with God's Holy Spirit.

…who came to enable us to become all we were meant to become.

Come . . . and Behold Him!

NIGHT LIKE NO OTHER

*When the fullness of time
had come, God sent forth His Son.*

GALATIANS 4:4

On this night without equal
      our God wrote a sequel
To man's hopeless legend of loss.
What began in a garden cried out for pardon,
God soon would provide through a Cross.
For that dear baby's crying now forecasts a dying,
His coming is planned to bring life
And this heaven-sent stranger now laid in a manger,
Is God come to heal
And God's love to reveal
God in flesh now appearing, Salvation is nearing
The earth-hope for peace now has come.
Open hearts now receive Him
Fear not to believe Him,
The Savior of man,
Here fulfilling God's plan
In the Person of Jesus has come.

Come . . . and Behold Him!

SEARCH MY HEART

Search me, O God, and know my heart: test my thoughts. Point out anything you find in me that makes you sad, and lead me along the path of everlasting life.

PSALM 139:23–24, TLB

David's earnest desire to walk before God with his whole heart is an unsurpassed example of what pleases God the most.

David's "open door policy" toward God teaches us a fundamental lesson: The purpose of having God search our hearts is so we may discover sin and confess it. This kind of openness—confessing sin without self-justifying debate—allows the Lord free entry to examine and correct us. We accept His dealings and agree with His assessments.

Our Daily Walk

Pathways of Blessing

*Show the path where I should go, O LORD; point
out the right road for me to walk. Lead me; teach me.*

PSALM 25:4–5, TLB

We can ask God for specific direction for
the day, and can expect Him to give us that
direction at crucial points if we stay open to Him.
And, though God doesn't want us to become
mystical or superstitious, we can expect Jesus to
direct us in ways that are custom-made, especially
designed to bless others and us in the process.

God promises to help us avoid serious
mistakes or errors. We can be confident He will
lead us down pathways of blessing and will keep us
walking a path of practical, good-sense living.

Our Daily Walk

GOD'S PURPOSE

*O LORD, I pray, please let Your ear be attentive
to the prayer of Your servant, and to the prayer of Your
servants who desire to fear Your name.*

NEHEMIAH 1:11

I have spoken with thousands of people who view their past and present failures as guarantees God will never be able to complete His purpose in their lives. For these people—indeed for most of us—a call to obedience seems a virtual seal against victory, for perfect obedience eludes them. But note the link this prayer forges between the heart and the intent to obey. What I *want* of God's will counts more than the achievement of what I've *done*.

1 Samuel 16:7 says, "Man looks at the outward appearance, but the LORD looks at the heart." God is not as concerned with our *perfection* as He is with our *direction*.

Rebuilding the Real You

THE PLEDGE OF HIS SPIRIT

"I will never leave you nor forsake you."

HEBREWS 13:5

 For you and me there will be times when we may feel the Savior is a million miles away from our situation. But receive the promise, dear one. He has placed His Spirit within you and me as a certified assurance of His will to complete everything! And until He settles all things and eventually takes us home to Himself, we may continually rely on the presence of the living God. No matter how dark or long your night, He has pledged, "I will never leave you nor forsake you!"

A New Time and Place

So Great a Savior

*You are God, ready to pardon, gracious
and merciful, slow to anger, abundant in kindness.*

NEHEMIAH 9:17

Let the new year be a year of growth and harvest!

—Growing in our walks with Jesus—staying close to Him.

—Growing in the Word of God—deepening in understanding.

—Growing in faith, prayer, and boldness in giving.

—Growing in loving, serving, and helping those we can.

There is nothing too great for us to expect since we have so great a Savior and Lord.

Come . . . and Behold Him!

THE PATTERN FOR WORSHIP

*To Him who loved us and washed us
from our sins in His own blood, and has made us
kings and priests to His God.*

REVELATION 1:5–6

These words supply a pattern for worship. First, this pattern exalts the *Person* we worship: Jesus, who died to redeem us from the sin curse of eternal death, and who did so at the expense of His own life-blood shed on the Cross.

Second, it qualifies the *practice* of our worship: a priestly ministry. We have a lifelong call (one never outgrows worship) and a holy calling (purity and piety are never options).

Third, it presents the *perspective* on worship: Kingship!

Worship His Majesty

As I'm kneeling here

with New Year drawing near

my hands extend to You

my heart is hungry, too,

for all that's old and new;

of all You call me to—

that naught be lost,

whate'er the cost,

that You will find me true.

ACKNOWLEDGMENTS

Grateful acknowledgment is made to the following publishers for permission to reprint this copyrighted material.

Eastman, Dick and Jack Hayford. *Living and Praying in Jesus' Name* (Wheaton, Illinois: Tyndale House, 1988).
Hayford, Jack. *Come . . . and Behold Him!* (Sisters, Oregon: Multnomah Publishing House, 1995).
————*How to Live Through a Bad Day* (Nashville, Tennessee: Thomas Nelson, 2001).
————*Glorious Morning!: The Invitation to Resurrection Praise* (Sisters, Oregon: Multnomah Publishing House, 1996).
————*Glory on Your House* (Grand Rapids, Michigan: Chosen Books, 1982).
————*Grounds for Living* (Grand Rapids, Michigan: Chosen Books, 2001).
————*The Heart of Praise: Daily Ways to Worship the Father with Psalms* (Ventura, California: Regal Books, 1992).
————*The Key to Everything* (Lake Mary, Florida: Charisma House, 1993).
————*The Leading Edge* (Lake Mary, Florida: Charisma House, 2001).
————*Living the Spirit-Formed Life* (Ventura, California: Regal Books, 2001).
————*Moments with Majesty* (Sisters, Oregon: Multnomah Publishing House, 1990).
————*A New Time and Place: Preparing Yourself to Receive God's Best* (Sisters, Oregon: Multnomah Publishing House, 1997).
————*Our Daily Walk* (Kent, England: Sovereign World, 1997).

———*A Passion for Fullness* (Fort Worth, Texas: LIFE Publishing, 1990).

———*Pastors of Promise* (Ventura, California: Regal Books, 1997)

———*The Power and Blessing* (Wheaton, Illinois: Victor Books, 1994).

———*Prayer Is Invading the Impossible* (Gainesville, Florida: Bridge-Logos, 1977).

———*Rebuilding the Real You* (Van Nuys, California: Jack Hayford Ministries, 2003).

———*Taking Hold of Tomorrow* (Ventura, California: Regal Books, 1989)

———*The Visitor* (Wheaton, Illinois: Tyndale House, 1986).

———*Worship His Majesty* (Nashville, Tennessee: W Publishing, 1987).

For information on obtaining Jack Hayford ministry materials currently in print call 800-776-8180 or visit www.jackhayford.com

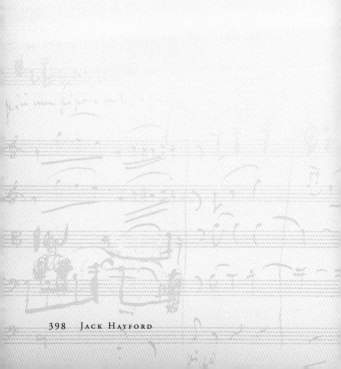

NOTES

NOTES